Praise for *Swingers: True Confessions from Today's Swinging Scene*

'discover who does it, where they go and what really happens'

Star on Sunday

'lifts the lid on the secretive world of swingers'

Daily Express

'new book uncovers secret sex craze sweeping Britain'

News of the World

ABOUT THE AUTHOR

Ashley Lister is a freelance writer, reporter and the author of *Swingers: True Confessions from Today's Swinging Scene*. Aside from writing erotic fiction under a variety of pseudonyms, Ashley's non-fiction has appeared in a wide range of magazines that include *Forum*, *The International Journal of Erotica* and *Chapter & Verse*. Ashley's full-length fiction includes more than two dozen novels, with shorter fiction appearing in a range of international anthologies and magazines.

SWINGERS: FEMALE CONFIDENTIAL

Ashley Lister

First published in 2008 by
Virgin Books
Thames Wharf Studios
Rainville Rd
London W6 9HA

A catalogue record of this book is available from
the British Library

ISBN 9780753513439

Random House Group Limited supports The Forest
Stewardship Council [FSC], the leading international forest
certification organisation. All our titles that are printed on
Greenpeace approved FSC certified paper carry the FSC logo.
Our paper procurement policy can be found at
www.rbooks.co.uk/environment

Design and typesetting by TW Typesetting, Plymouth, Devon

Printed and bound in Great Britain by
CPI Bookmarque, Croydon, CR0 4TD

1 3 5 7 9 10 8 6 4 2

I wouldn't have been able to write this book without contributions from the countless remarkable ladies who shared their time, thoughts and memories. However, I would never have been able to write anything if not for the love and support of one singularly remarkable lady: thank you, Tracy.

CONTENTS

INTRODUCTION

> **Author Needs to Talk** with female
> swingers. Married or single, I want to find
> out how you swing and, most importantly,
> why you swing. Discretion assured. P.O.
> Box AL000

Following the publication of *Swingers: True Confessions from Today's Swinging Scene*, I've been asked many questions. This means I either didn't write the book properly or the people talking to me are just too curious for their own good. Many people want to know how the parties are organised; who goes to them; and what I did while I was there. If the answers to those questions aren't in the previous book, you can guarantee they're either not important, or they're floating around somewhere on the internet.

But the commonest question, the one most frequently posed, is: *Why do women swing?*

Swinging, for the purposes of this book and its predecessor, is a blanket term used to cover those incidents within relationships where established couples consent to their partners having sexual encounters with others. These encounters range from mild flirtations, kissing and exhibitionism through to full penetrative sex, orgies, dogging and gangbangs. I've elected to use the term as a blanket reference rather than relying on an established definition because the milieu of swinging is personal to each participant and there are few singles or couples who would agree on what constitutes a swinger or swinging. In truth, within the swinging community, few couples *swing*: they '*play*', they '*share*', or they '*party*'. Rather than being members of the swinging community many are '*part of the scene*', others '*live the lifestyle*', and the remainder are '*just doing their own thing*'.

Strangely, I have started several interviews for this book (and its predecessor) hearing the disconcerting statement, 'I don't think you really want to talk to us. We're not swingers. We're just a married couple who have sex with lots of other people.' This has happened so many times it does suggest the term *swinging* may have many negative connotations. It also implies that there is an undiscovered subset of promiscuous adults in the UK; a subset who will never consider swinging, swapping or sharing as long as they are able, as a couple, to continue having extra-marital sex inside and outside their existing relationship.

All of this is stated to show that my choice to simplify the language is not an arbitrary decision or done to reinforce any negative connotations associated with the terms *swingers* or *swinging*. I have chosen to use the popular terminology in an attempt to keep this text comparatively clear and free from unnecessary ambiguity.

Although the accuracy of statistics is hard to verify, the oft-quoted figure that there are a million swingers in the UK does not seem like an exaggeration. Totalling the membership figures of the UK's clubs and websites (dividing it appropriately to allow for a percentage of duplicates, and allowing for a variable to account for those swingers who don't use clubs, members-only bars or the internet) the figure is still close to a million. If you take into account the couples I mentioned before, who don't identify themselves as swingers but still have a sex life that most people would define as swinging, then the number is much, much higher.

And the numbers are constantly increasing.

As mentioned in this book's predecessor, the age range of swingers stretches across a broad spectrum but with a heavier concentration of figures in the groups of late thirties and early forties.

In the 1980s and 1990s it was comparatively common for sociologists and psychologists to profile swingers as an example of a deviant culture. These studies (neatly summarised in Richard J Jenks's 1998 article, 'Swinging: A Review of the Literature'[1]) proved little except what was already quite apparent: i.e. swingers are virtually indistinguishable from other members of society except for their participation in recreational sex. Being described as mainly middle class, their political attitudes and opinions remained consistent with their income. The only area where swingers were deemed notably deviant in their responses was in their liberal attitude towards sex and sexuality. All of which paints a broad portrait of swingers as anonymous members of our general communities. The only honest conclusion one can draw from these results is an understanding as to why further sociological studies have not been commissioned.

To be fair, the surveys mentioned in Jenks's article did throw up one notable difference between the swinging and non-swinging population. Bartell (1971), Gilmartin (1975)

---

[1] Jenks, R.J. (1998), 'Swinging: A Review of the Literature', *Archives of Sexual Behavior* (pages 507 +), Volume 27, Issue 5, Plenum Publishing Corporation, New York.

and Jenks (1985) all report that the majority of swingers surveyed '. . . did not attend church regularly' and '. . . had no present religious identification'. The figures in these surveys range from sixty-three per cent through to seventy per cent of respondents, which contrasts starkly with poles of the non-swinging community where Gallup and Castelli (1989) show ninety-two per cent of respondents claim a religious preference.

It's difficult to know what to make of this disparity.

An overview of religious texts would suggest a tendency to demonise all sex that is not explicitly intended for the purpose of procreation. I Corinthians (7: 18) advises: 'Flee from sexual immorality.' And this comes immediately after a rant against idolaters, adulterers, male prostitutes and homosexual offenders. Galatians (6: 19–21) similarly warns against sexual immorality, impurity and debauchery, specifically mentioning orgies, before going on to warn '. . . that those who live like this will not inherit the kingdom of God.' Admittedly, Genesis is replete with illicit couplings and matrimonially sanctioned adultery but it's widely accepted most Bible-based religions interpret these parts of the Good Book to suit their own particular agenda.

To illustrate this point it should be noted that the majority of Christian religions vehemently deny accusations of being institutionally sexist. And yet the Millennium edition of The New Testament (the most recently revised version of the Christian Bible) still includes unexpurgated instructions from *Peter* (3: 1) 'Wives [. . .] be submissive to your husbands . . .' This attitude can be deemed patriarchal in the kindest light although it would be easy to see how others may construe it as downright misogynistic. Consequently, with religions tailoring the intent of the Bible's message to suit their own arguments, it's easy to accept why those who want to enjoy recreational sex would not want to suffer sermons condemning them for their prurient interests.

However, sociology and religion aside, the original question I've been posed still remains unanswered: *Why do women swing?*

It says a lot about our society that no one asks why men swing. Clearly the majority of people are in accord that the answer to that one is a no-brainer. Men swing because there is an opportunity for extra sex, and that in itself is sufficient motivation. I don't personally subscribe to this solution. I believe men swing for a variety of reasons. Admittedly, one of those reasons will often be the opportunity for more sex, but men's motivations aren't limited to the generalisation of that one simple answer. Some men swing because it gives them and their partners an opportunity for greater pleasure. Some men swing because it provides an acceptable outlet for their bisexuality while they continue to maintain an otherwise satisfying heterosexual relationship. Some men swing because the social element appeals to them. Some men swing simply because they're married to a partner who swings and both are happy with the dynamics of an open relationship.

But, regardless of men's reasons, their motives are seldom questioned. No one has yet asked me why men swing. It's far more likely people want to know: *Why do women swing?*

This enquiry, possibly a twenty-first century variant on Freud's most sexist lament, 'What do women want?' was approached in several ways. But it always boils down to the same thing.

- What's a woman's motive for swinging?
- Are women really happy swinging?
- What do women get out of swinging?

- Are women being forced into swinging against their will?
- Do women only swing because their husbands can't satisfy them?

In the following pages I will attempt to address these questions and other related issues. I've communicated with a wide range of open-minded females who either swing; have swung; intend to swing; or have a relevant opinion on the whole subject of swinging and recreational sex. I've chatted with singles, couples, married, widowed, divorced, heterosexual, bisexual and lesbian women. I've talked with lawyers, porn stars, tax collectors, retired housewives and first-year undergraduates. In short, I've talked with a lot of women and the results of those many, many conversations are contained in the following pages.

And, while I don't think there is a single definitive response, I hope this book ultimately gives a clearer answer to the question: *Why do women swing?*

Ashley Lister, 2008

FIRST TIMERS

For this chapter, I've chosen examples from an eclectic range of swingers covering a broad spectrum of ages, opinions and attitudes. Anecdotal evidence would suggest that a large majority of swingers become involved with recreational sex through a similar route. Many have been in established relationships for a decade or more before they consider swinging. The impetus for these couples is often an unexpected freedom (i.e. children leaving home, a change of occupation, alteration of circumstances, etc.) that allows them the opportunity to explore the reality of long-cherished fantasies. Usually the subject of swinging or swapping or sharing is discussed; first as a sexual fantasy and then as a potential reality; the potential pros and cons are weighed and argued; and then, if they're still interested in exploring the lifestyle, the couple go through the tenuous processes of initiation and experimentation.

In researching this book I have spoken to many couples who fitted loosely into the aforementioned category. I have also spoken with couples who were in an open relationship that has been complemented by the experience of swinging. I've spoken to some that have found swinging a convenient outlet for their bisexuality. And I've chatted with others who've returned to swinging years after a pleasurable group experience that occurred before they were settled in a relationship. I have also interviewed several couples who chose to explore recreational sex to compensate for a routine, mundane or unsatisfactory love life.

However, regardless of anyone's motives for swinging, everyone who has ever participated in swinging has had a memorable first experience.

Amy is a slender brunette who, when she swings, favours full-length crotchless body-stockings that complement the curves of her svelte figure. She looks considerably younger than her forty-three years and has been married for twenty-four years to Richard. The couple have two teenage children and live near Manchester where she works as a medical receptionist.
Throughout their twenty-four-year marriage Amy estimates that she has slept with approximately five hundred men. Her husband knows about each of these encounters and lovingly supports and encourages his wife's voracious sexual appetite.

Amy: 'Before I got married I was always very promiscuous. I was never faithful to any of my boyfriends. I enjoy sex and I always have done. I reach orgasm fairly easily and I do like the sensation of having an orgasm. When I met Richard I fell in love and I didn't want to be unfaithful to him. He knew I'd been around a bit but he accepted me for who I was – not who I'd been with or what I'd done – and I was prepared to make a fresh start. I remained faithful through-out the whole twelve months that we were engaged. But I ended up fucking another man only six weeks after we got married.'

Amy reaches for Richard's hand as she speaks and squeezes as she continues. Her brow is creased with obvious consternation. 'We got married in the November. Six weeks later we were at a New Year's Eve party. As the party started to warm up the host asked me to help him get some drinks from the garage. Within two minutes of being alone he had my skirt up and he was fucking me against the garage wall. It was just raw sex. Nothing particularly special. No foreplay. Nothing exciting.

'But Richard caught us.

'I was very worried at first. I panicked. I loved Richard. I do still love Richard. And I hadn't wanted to do something so foolish that was going to hurt him. But I have a wandering eye. Well, if it was just my eye that wandered there wouldn't have been a problem. The twelve months of our engagement had been easy at first because we were so much in love. But it became a lot harder for me as the months wore on. If I'm being honest with myself I'm surprised I lasted as long as I did before I fucked another man.

'I expected Richard would be upset and angry. I thought my foolishness would mean an end to our marriage. And I didn't think it would be possible to have a worse end to the old year or a bleaker beginning to the new one. It came as quite a surprise when Richard explained how much me being with another man had excited him. He'd followed us into the garage because he'd suspected I was going to do something with the party's host. He'd also watched for a while before interrupting.'

After passing her husband a reassuring glance, Amy finally releases her hold on Richard's hand. As she smiles, the creases ease from her brow. 'The sex we had that night was out of this world. The following day was New Year's Day and it really was the best way to start the New Year.

'Of course, we had a long discussion.

'I had no idea Richard was OK about me going with other men. I never suspected that he wanted me to go with other men. But when we were honest and communicating about our needs and our desires, that was when the floodgates opened. The conversation we had that night set the course of our relationship. Richard said it was fine for me to have sex with whoever I wanted, as long as I was safe and as long as I let him know every detail.

'The main thing, from our point of view, is that sex and making love are two totally different things. I make love with Richard. I have sex with other men. Of course there are times when I have sex with Richard too, and that can be really good. But I never make love to anyone else. Only Richard.

'Once a week, sometimes more if the urge is on me, sometimes less if it's school holidays or we've got holidays or other plans, I'll go out to a local club or pub. I very rarely try and pick men up, I've never had any problems waiting for men to approach me and make the first move. It always happens.

'Well, ninety-nine per cent of the time it happens.

'After a couple of drinks, and maybe a dance or two, I'll let him take me back to his place. And then we'll fuck. I usually try and take pictures while we're doing it. That way I can share the experience more fully with Richard when I get home. Usually I'm pretty focused on what I'm doing with the bloke who's picked me up. But if I get a good snapshot of, say, me sucking his cock or him penetrating me, then I'll get more aroused as I think about the excitement Richard's going to get from seeing the picture.'

Going to her computer monitor, Amy calls up a series of pictures that show her with a variety of partners. She explains that the pictures represent a very small portion of her collection. They have captured scenes of brightly exciting sexual imagery. Different penises are visible on most of the pictures. They appear in a range of shapes, sizes and colours: from black and white through to red and purple. Some are in Amy's hand, others between her buttocks, against her breasts or half-hidden because the picture was taken while they were penetrating her vagina. Some of the pictures show the half-hidden faces of different men; several of them locked against the split in one of Amy's many crotchless body-stockings. The majority of pictures show Amy's lips around unsheathed erections.

'Richard prefers pictures of my mouth around another man's cock,' Amy explains. 'I use protection – condoms – whenever I'm having sex. I always use condoms whenever I'm having sex. But I don't use them for oral. They taste vile. And I don't think they're necessary for oral sex.'

It's tempting to interrupt, and advise that contemporary research on the use of condoms shows that, even with oral sex, they reduce the risk of contracting many STDs. But Amy is talking quickly and the opportunity to make the point passes.

'I think that's what Richard likes seeing. I think he likes the sight of my lips and tongue touching the bare skin of another man's cock. Which is fine with me. I enjoy oral – giving and receiving. I could happily have a man licking me while I suck his cock all night. It's a shame more men aren't better at giving oral but, when I find one who is good, I make sure I get as much out of him as he can give.

'And I always try to take pictures so Richard can see what I've been doing when we make love afterwards. For him, and for me, that's the best part of the experience. He gets so excited knowing I've been fucking someone else. He gets so excited when I'm telling him how they were touching me and what we were doing together. I get just as aroused because, for me, it's like I'm reliving the experience with the man I love.

'For me it's like having the proverbial cake and eating it.

'I think we're able to do this because we're very much in love. We don't argue as a couple and it's not because I'm domineering or he's henpecked. He's a very strong man and he's above emotions like jealousy. We don't argue because, when you love someone, you don't argue. Richard is comfortable that I go out once, sometimes twice, each week.' Amy glances at Richard for confirmation and he nods agreement. 'Like I said before: it excites him and he's happy to be aroused by my experiences.

'I don't know if five hundred is an accurate number but I do think the figure is somewhere round there. I've been seeing other men on a regular basis throughout most of our marriage. I stopped seeing other men while I was pregnant. Both times. Those times were special. Those times were just for me and Richard. And I never have sex when it's my time of the month. I never feel in the mood.

'There have also been some men that I've seen more than once.

'I've recently dumped one man who I'd been fucking occasionally for the past five years. I got bored with him. He managed to hold my interest for five years, which is a lot longer than most of these men can manage. Usually I've had enough of them after one night. So he lasted well. But, as always happens with sex partners, I got bored with him.

'I suppose it's because I get bored so easily that I go through men so quickly. I have lust issues. Unless a man can show me something new, exciting or fun, he doesn't hold my interest. I'm pretty open-minded about most things sexually. I won't do scat or pain – well, not serious pain. I'm all right with having a man bite my nipples, maybe give me a few rough caresses or try some anal fingering, but I don't like to be hurt. I'm into pleasure, not pain. Because my five-year man liked to experiment, I was quite comfortable seeing him regularly. And it was exciting while it lasted. But that one's definitely over now.' She nods her head emphatically and says again, 'That one's definitely over now. I know that Richard wishes he could watch me more. He's only seen me with other men a handful of times. There are so few men who are willing to allow another man to watch them while they're fucking. Especially while they're fucking that man's wife. But I do try to include Richard as much as I can whenever I can.

'Quite recently we met up with a man from the internet who thought he'd be able to manage it. He'd made all sorts of outrageous promises online about the things he could do for me and to me. And he said it was no problem if Richard was there, watching, because he'd show him how to do the job properly. He was full of bravado and bluster. But, when we met up, nerves had got the better of him. He didn't "measure up" the way he'd boasted and he couldn't get an erection, no matter how hard I tried for him. Instead of this bloke fucking me while Richard watched, it ended up the other way round. Richard fucked me while this poor bloke just sat there – watching and looking mortified.

'Not that I'm a great fan of having more than one man at a time. I've had a couple of threesomes, and been the centre of attention while two men fucked me – one after the other.' She grins slyly: an expression that suggests the experiences weren't entirely unpleasant. 'But I prefer the one-on-one situation. I find it easier to concentrate on one man at a time.'

On the subject of how long she plans to continue swinging, Amy says, 'I'm going to carry on seeing other men until I'm fifty. It's getting more awkward now that the kids are older. They're both teenagers and, whenever I go out, they keep asking, "Where are you going, Mum?" I'm sure they believe the excuses I give them but I don't like having to lie to my kids.

'But they're not the reason why I intend to stop when I reach fifty. I think, when a woman reaches fifty, it's an age where she should be acting with some dignity and maturity – and those aren't words you associate with a woman who sees a different bloke every other week. Richard thinks the decision is sensible. And we'll always have the pictures that I've taken over the years. Whenever I want to relive my glory days I'll always be able to look through those photos and remember how much fun it is to have your cake and eat it.'

Beryl and Brian have been married for thirty-three years and swinging for one. Beryl is a fifty-one-year-old tax collector from Essex. She has shoulder-length blonde hair and an athletic figure that she maintains with regular trips to the gym. In their single year of swinging they seem to have managed more than many similarly-inclined couples achieve in a decade or more. Together they are a personable couple who take a lot of pleasure from their involvement in the swinging lifestyle.

Beryl: 'We've tried every method of swinging. But we prefer parties and clubs, including spa clubs. We both indulge in full swap, same room and group sex.' Beryl makes these admissions with an enthusiasm that is obvious and irre-pressible. Her enjoyment of the swinging lifestyle is blatant and infectious. 'Just over a year ago Brian was secretly looking at live internet web cams. He was always up late at night and rarely went to bed at the same time as me, despite my requests. I had a feeling that he'd either lost interest in our relationship or was seeing someone else. I tackled the subject by openly asking. He said that he was turned on by what he saw on the internet, but assured me there was nobody else involved.'

Beryl admits that this conversation was a turning point and opened up the floodgates for the first honest exchange of fantasies in their entire marriage. 'I told him I'd often fantasised about having sex with other people. Throughout our marriage I've been monogamous and faithful to Brian. I'd never acted on my fantasies, or even mentioned my desire for a varied and adventurous sex life. This was the first time we'd ever had such a frank and open discussion. Having sex with other people was something I'd always wanted but never experienced before. I was a virgin when I married Brian and I was growing desperately curious to explore other avenues.

'Within two weeks of talking about it we visited our first spa club. We went to a place called Rio's. The club permits nudity and I found myself naked in a steam room with Brian and two strangers. That was exciting in itself. I'd been aroused on the journey down there. I was very aroused when I found myself naked with these two men so close. And then, when Brian excused himself and I realised I was naked and alone with these two men, the excitement really did kick in.' Beryl blushes as she recalls this incident. But, because the blush is coupled with a bright, self-satisfied expression, it's apparent that the experience wasn't unpleasant.

'One of them said, "I haven't seen you here before."

'I told him, "I haven't been here before."

'The other said, "So, is this your first time?"

'They both seemed very interested when I said, "Yes."

'They were leaning closer, touching me, and letting me touch them. Because I knew that was why we had gone there, I didn't have any reservations about starting. I was only a little bit nervous on those first few occasions.

'One of them had his mouth against my breast while he sucked at my nipple. The other pushed his cock in my hand and started to touch me down there. At Rio's, in the steam room, I ended up masturbating both men as one of them fingered me to a climax. The experience left me hungry for more. It was the first time I'd touched any man's cock, other than Brian's. It was the first time any man, other than Brian, had touched me down there.

'It really was a revelation.

'Once we'd started swinging there seemed to be no stopping us. Within a fortnight we'd arranged to meet a swinging couple and we'd enjoyed our first full swap. That really was exciting for me. Until that point the only man I'd ever had proper sex with was Brian. Even though I'd masturbated those two men in the steam room, I'd not properly had sex with anyone else. And, from that point, I just wanted to experience more and more.' It's hard to imagine the woman Beryl is talking about. She has spent a year becoming a confident and impassioned swinger and the transformation looks like it is almost complete. She dresses with the confidence a woman who knows she is sexy. She holds herself with the poise of a woman who likes to flirt – and then go further. As Beryl talks about the person she was before she became a swinger, the woman she was when she had only ever known Brian, it's easier to imagine that she's talking about a completely different person.

'We mostly use the net for meeting other couples,' Beryl explains.

'We've met up with a few single men too and that's been a great social experience as well as a sexual one. We'll see some of these men when we're not planning to have sex together and then, at the end of the evening, one thing will invariably lead to another and we'll end up in bed together.' The laughter that follows this statement echoes with the ring of mischievous satisfaction.

'The whole year has been a rush from one new experience to another and each one just seems better than the one before. Shortly after we started we went to a club in the Costa del Sol. We'd been swinging for about four months then. There were several large playrooms. The beds were big enough for six to eight people. And there were lots of people there. It didn't take long for me to get into the mood to join in.

'I was giving oral sex to two Spanish men at the same time.

'Behind me another couple were having full sex. They were both young and quite vigorous. They kept changing positions with the male leading and pulling his partner around quite a lot. She'd been in the club's spa and she was tossing her wet hair around. Spray from it kept splashing everywhere. The two Spanish men had been touching me while I sucked them and I was beginning to get very aroused. There were at least another six people in the room watching and it was all very exciting.

'The passionate couple who had been writhing together and changing positions every two minutes stopped very suddenly. In an instant the girl had moved off from her partner and pulled me away from the two Spanish men I was sucking. She laid me across one of the huge playroom beds in full view of everyone watching.

'This was my first experience of sex with another woman. The two Spaniards I'd been sucking followed and they continued to masturbate while this woman went down on me.

'I came to orgasm in seconds.

'While I was writhing and groaning through my climax the two Spaniards both ejaculated over my naked body. I was left on the playroom bed trembling, stunned and extremely satisfied. The surprise and explosiveness of the situation left me in a shell-shocked state. Having both these men ejaculate on me was a thrill. But I loved the surprise element of the female involvement. That was something I'd always wanted to experience and it was a wonderful introduction to the pleasures of what sex can be like with a woman.'

That first experience in Spain was enough to earn a special place in Beryl's affections. Along with her husband, Beryl has been able to observe the swinging cultures in the UK and those in Europe, and she believes there are obvious differences in the approach of the participants. 'The atmospheres aren't comparable,' she explains. 'UK swinging clubs are generally populated by a more reserved clientele. Swingers in the UK are usually concentrating more on the social side of swinging. On the continent it's very different. People there just go for it. There's so much more passion.' She refutes the suggestion that her observations could be overlooking some key issues. Yes, there is a language barrier that makes socialising more difficult. Yes, she had experienced continental swinging while enjoying a relaxing holiday. But she still maintains the continental clubs are far more passionate than their UK counterparts.

'One of the other things we've noticed with continental swinging is male masturbation plays a big part in the experience. In the swinging quarter of France's Cap d'Agde we often saw groups of men happily, and unselfconsciously, masturbating. Usually these men were watching a couple play together, and once or twice watching a lone woman playing with herself. But it's far more common to see men masturbating abroad than it is to see that at swingers' parties in the UK. I think I like that unselfconsciousness. I like the fact that they have so few inhibitions.' The way she stresses this final sentence makes it clear that this is what

Beryl enjoys most about her own swinging. Beryl has discovered a lifestyle without inhibitions and she clearly loves every moment.

Chelsea is attractive, twenty years old, dark-skinned, with a tall, willowy figure. Her measurements are 32D with a 28" waist and 36" hips. She is a full-time student in the north of England and swings with her on/off partner Martin, twenty-three years her senior. Chelsea divides her free time between swingers' and fetish parties, the latter of which she describes as, 'Swingers' parties with clothes.' Chelsea's first swinging experience occurred when she was eighteen years old.

Chelsea: 'About a month into our relationship, Martin and I were in bed one evening and we were talking about things that we were into. It turned out to be a pretty extensive list. We're both bisexual. And we're open-minded enough to try most things. As the discussion went on I said I'd watched a documentary a while ago and they were due to repeat it that evening. It was some documentary on real-life swingers or real-life wife swaps on Channel 5. When I'd first seen it, it had a profound effect on me. The idea of being at a sex party with other adults had opened something in me. Ever since I'd first seen the programme, going to one of those parties had been something that I desperately wanted.

'I asked Martin, "Do you want to watch it tonight?" And we watched it together. And I said, "I've always thought about doing this."

'And he said, "I've done it."

'I was like, "Really! Wow! Fantastic! Would you ever do it again?"'

Chelsea explains that the last venue Martin had visited was Club Lash in Manchester, a fetish bar he'd attended with his ex. Martin admitted that he loved the atmosphere of Club Lash, and the decadence of the parties he'd been to before then. But he hadn't been to a party in five years. 'He got settled down with a boring woman,' Chelsea continues, 'and she wasn't into it. But they were no longer together. Martin had wanted to suggest parties to me before but, because I was so much younger than him, and I think he saw me as being naïve or innocent, he hadn't wanted to make such a bold suggestion. So we both said, "Let's do it. Let's find out some places where we could go."'

With a wicked smile she bats her lashes and adds, 'About three weeks later, we did it. Martin learnt about a local club that was hosting a party. He got in touch with the owners, found out some details and we agreed to go. Looking back on that night it was just a fantastic first venue. A good experience.'

Shaking her head, looking as though she is trying to reconcile conflicting thoughts, Chelsea says, 'I was absolutely terrified,' then adds: 'It was fantastic.' She laughs at her own indecisiveness and spends a few moments talking about how hard it is to describe her emotions. It was both good and bad. Exciting and frightening. Wholly wanted, yet totally daunting. 'It was a time for a lot of firsts for me, so I can understand why Martin thought I was naïve and innocent. I'd never dressed up for anyone before. I'd never bought an outfit for myself before and I'd certainly never bought one for an adult party before. I'd never bought any outfit especially for sex – other than bits of lingerie and underwear – so I really was a virgin to all these new situations.

'The venue was advertised as a fetish party but I understood that meant it was just a swingers' party with clothes. I said I'd not got an outfit to go in, and Martin said I should just go in underwear. But I thought, if I want to do this, I want to do it right.

'I've always been a big fan of Dita Von Teese, the burlesque fetish-wear model,' Chelsea explains. Chelsea interrupts our conversation to show me her copy of *Burlesque and the Art of the Teese/Fetish and the Art of the Teese*. The book is a collection of photographs showing Dita Von Teese in a variety of glamorous costumes and poses. Watching the way Chelsea handles this treasured hardback, it's easy to understand that she reveres Dita Von Teese. 'She was Marilyn Manson's wife for a while,' Chelsea explains. 'She's my idol for all things fetish. I suppose she's my idol for everything. When Martin and me later went to the Torture Garden in London her pictures were all over the walls. There were screens in quite a few of the rooms, and they were constantly showing pictures of her. She's just absolutely stunning. So, with this being advertised as a fetish party, I wanted to go dressed the way I thought Dita Von Teese would go dressed. I wanted to do it right.

'So, I went to a local adult store and bought a leatherette bra and thong and some fishnet hold-ups. The outfit wasn't particularly outrageous, looking back on it. But it was my first time at a party of any type and, wearing those things, I felt as though I looked the part. I'd got the red lipstick, I was going for the whole burlesque image, and the whole experience of dressing up like Dita felt right. I could have worn a rubber dress. Martin had found out that there would be women there wearing little rubber dresses and stuff, and we figured they'd all be looking pretty sexy. And I can wear a rubber dress. I've got the figure for them and I've worn them to nightclubs because everything on your body is covered up. But I wanted to wear something more revealing. I wanted to be wearing the most revealing outfit at the party.

'As it turned out: I was.'

Chelsea carefully puts Dita's book away before continuing. 'It was an experience,' she says. 'I wore a coat over the leatherette bra, thong and fishnets. We met the owners at the door when we got there. Because they knew it was my first time, and I was quite young compared to their usual customers, they'd said I could keep my coat on and nothing would be said. But I said, "Nah! Fuck it. I'll just take it off."

'But it was still intimidating. The woman that runs the place, Louise, wore this skin-tight little rubber dress. She looked fantastic. Martin wore a PVC all-in-one bodysuit with a hole for his pierced nipple and a hole for his cock – which was hidden by the thong he wore over the bodysuit. So he was all covered up. The owner, Aaron, was all covered up inside a sarong. And I'm thinking, *Fuck! I'm just wearing underwear here! I'm so exposed. My tits and my arse are hanging out. I've got no clothes on.* Martin must have guessed what I was thinking because he said, "Don't worry. You won't stand out. I'll bet everyone else is wearing something similar to what you're wearing."' Chelsea laughs and adds, 'I was thinking, *I will stand out. I'm determined to.*

'So I took my coat off and walked in just wearing the leatherette bra and thong and the hold-ups. And I'm glad I did that. Everybody turned and looked when I walked in. I could see all of the men were just thinking, "Wow!" There was a buzz that came from making my entrance in such an eye-catching way. It was a buzz that just wouldn't have been there otherwise.

'The party had started at nine but we didn't get there until eleven.

'All of the people there were a hell of a lot more covered up than me. The women were wearing dresses mainly and, although I was buzzing from all the attention, I was still feeling a little awkward. Even so, when I went to the bar with Martin to get a drink, this short, cute guy did tell me I'd got a lovely arse.

'Not that I drank much while I was there. I'd said, from day one, "The first party I go to I don't want to be drunk. I want to feel what it's like while I'm completely sober. I only want to do the things that I would do sober. Not the things that I would do when I was drunk."' She reflects on this for a moment before confiding, 'I don't think there is much more that I'd do when I've had a drink. But I wanted to experience the party properly and soberly.

'So, we'd walked into the place and all eyes were on me. I was the most scantily dressed woman at the party. I was the youngest woman at the party. And – while it may sound arrogant – I was the most desirable woman at the party. As soon as I'd accepted that I was the centre of attention, from that point onwards I was like, "Oh yes! Bring it on." My nervousness disappeared and the night was just fantastic.

'Once we'd got a drink Aaron and Louise came and started chatting to us. They showed us around the venue, giving us a quick tour of the playrooms, explaining where the loos were, and then showing us the dungeons they had downstairs. Once we'd seen everything they took us back to the main room and left us on our own. Automatically, we sat down so we could get a good view of the big screen with the porn they were playing. Martin said, "Let's park ourselves in front of that for now and see how the evening develops."

'It gave us a chance to watch something horny while we checked out the other people at the party. We chatted briefly with two girls who were sisters. They'd come to the party with their bisexual best friend. They were pleasant enough but the sisters were only interested in me and not Martin and we told them that we came as a package.' Chelsea frowns ruefully as she explains, 'That was one of the things we'd agreed on before setting foot inside the party.

'Then there was a woman called Adele and her husband, we called him "*The Missing Link*". Adele's probably in her fifties, her early fifties. She isn't a stunner but she was as rude as hell – in the best way possible – and she had the attitude of a born dominatrix. She commanded attention with everything she said and did and I thought she was fantastic. Her husband, *The Missing Link*, he wasn't quite as appealing. Bless him. He seemed like a nice guy. But he didn't have any conversational skills. He kept apologising after everything he said, explaining that he was worried in case he'd said something that might offend me. I was thinking, *I'm at a swingers' party and only wearing leatherette underwear: I've come here to be offended.*

'I told Adele it was my first time and explained I was an innocent. I said I was a virgin to the whole party scene. I said that in a loud enough voice so that everyone heard. Then Martin and I left the main party room and went downstairs to one of the dungeons. We said we were just going down there for another look but I don't think anyone believed that.

'The dungeon was pretty much what I'd expected. There was a surgical table in the middle. The walls were black, decorated with Manga-esque pictures of fetish-type things, as well as chains and cuffs. Martin and me got on the surgical table and we were fucking for a while, enjoying the fact that we were somewhere new – somewhere different and exciting. And then somebody came into the room while we were fucking.

'I recognised him as the guy who'd told me I had a nice arse when I was at the bar. Like I said, he was a little guy. He was very cute. A really nice guy, as it turned out.

'Martin had me bent over the surgical table then. He was still being really considerate, still trying to protect me, and still acting like I was naïve and innocent. He whispered in my ear and asked, "What do you reckon? Should we ask him to join us?"

'I said, "Yeah! Let's."

'And that was all it took!' Chelsea laughs at this exclamation, seeming surprised that becoming a swinger had been so painless and easy. 'Martin invited him over and within seconds I was sucking off this short guy while Martin fucked me from behind. It was incredibly arousing. That's what I'd gone to the party for and I was delighted that things were working out as I'd hoped.

'The only problem was, Martin was still treating me too gently. To put that right I took the short guy's cock out of my mouth, looked straight at Martin and said, "Right! Swap!"

'Martin did a double take at first and then, I could see from his eyes, he was thinking, "Oh my god! She's not innocent and naïve. She's a slut!" I think that was the most exciting point of the evening for Martin. It's certainly the incident he keeps mentioning whenever we talk about parties.

'So, Martin and the short guy swapped round. For the first time in our relationship, I've got my boyfriend's cock in my mouth while a stranger is fucking me. And, because everyone in the main room had seen the most attractive girl in the room head for the dungeon, they all seemed to follow.

'Adele and *The Missing Link* came in first. She asked, "Can we play?" I said, "Yes," and changed position so I was laid on the surgical table with Adele on top of me, and fingering me. Like I said, she wasn't a stunner, but she was very rude and very dominating. I was quite submissive at the time and her domination was a huge turn-on for me. Martin stepped back for a moment and then *The Missing Link* stepped forward to see if I'd suck his cock. But he didn't do anything for me so I told him to get off. In fairness, he was quite polite about it, and accepted what I said without question.

'One of the sisters I'd been chatting to earlier came over next. She was absolutely stunning. Gorgeous. She was in a PVC dress that was off the shoulder at one side. She explained that the short cute guy I was fucking was her bisexual best friend. She asked if she and her sister could join me on the table and I said that definitely wasn't a problem. I had Adele and these two birds on me, the cute short guy was still fucking me, and Martin was somewhere in the background taking photographs.'

In the majority of swingers' clubs and bars photography is not permissible. When this is mentioned to Chelsea she flexes an embarrassed grin and explains that Martin was quite insistent that he was going to take pictures regardless of whether anyone minded or not. His one concession to the rules was to insist, if a person didn't want to be photographed, they should move away from Chelsea who was the centre of all his pictures. When the owners visited the dungeon they accepted Martin could take photographs of Chelsea as long as whoever was with her knew that pictures were being taken.

'We've got some grotesque pictures of that evening. Martin took shots of me from various angles and none of them are very flattering. There are pictures where I'm beneath six or seven bodies, all of them naked and writhing around on top of me. I don't think anyone can look seductive in that situation. The pictures Martin took were basically me, wet, open with someone on top of me, or inside me, or both. Not very flattering pictures,' she concedes honestly. Then, with a flash of characteristic arrogance she adds, 'But because they've got me in them, I suppose they're the best pictures you can have really.

'We ended up leaving the party about three o'clock in the morning. I think I realised then that the evening had been all about me and hardly about Martin at all. He told me afterwards that he had started to fuck Adele but she was very domineering and he's not into that. Adele was telling him he's not allowed to come until she gives him permission, and Martin wasn't having any of that. His attitude is, "If I'm coming, I'm coming." So he and Adele realised they'd got incompatible attitudes and they left it at that. I think he might have been a bit bored just getting to fuck me a couple of times, half-fuck Adele, and then taking a load of pictures. But, while it wasn't a great night for him, I think that was probably the best first experience I could have had.

'When people chatted I got to know their names, and the atmosphere was very friendly. It's not what I'm looking for now. I prefer a much more hardcore experience nowadays. But, as an introduction to swinging – when I was nervous, naïve and innocent – it set my mind at ease. It was perfect.'

SINGLE BI FEMALE

> **Single Bi Female** looking to meet the
> right couple for 3sum fun. Only letters with
> photos will get replies. P.O. Box AL002

In the swinging world it seems that almost everyone is
searching for the SBF – Single Bi Female. Married men want
her to complete the FMF [Female/Male/Female] threesome
they dream of enjoying. Married women need her to explore
the bisexual fantasies they harbour. Demand for the SBF is
so great that every other swinger's contact ad on the
internet begs for her to respond. Swingers' clubs in the UK
offer her drastically discounted admission or welcome her
through their doors free of charge. Yet sightings of the SBF
are so rare there are many people who believe she is nothing
more than an urban myth.

Researching this book I've met with several of these urban
myths and I can confirm that, although they are few in
number, they do exist. Yet it's easy to understand why their
existence is so often called into question. It's also easy to
understand why the SBF is such a rare and seldom-met breed.

In many ways 'single swinging' is more easily accom-
plished by men than women.

Single male swingers are often nervous meeting strangers on their own, or entering swingers' parties unaccompanied. But society has conditioned men to meet this challenge. Most men feel comfortable going to a non-swinging pub or club without a companion. Even if they don't feel entirely comfortable, they strive to appear undaunted by the prospect and these attitudes transfer easily from the non-swinging world through to the lifestyle of swingers. Most men believe themselves capable of dealing with unexpected situations that might arise when they are out alone because self-reliance and independence have been traditionally encouraged as desirable masculine qualities. And it's widely agreed that most men are able to spin accusations of their promiscuity into confirmation of their virility and desirability.

But these attitudes seldom apply to women. Many women, swingers and non-swingers, feel awkward entering a bar alone. And, although society's attitude towards female sexuality is slowly changing, there continues to be a two-tier disparity that praises the 'stud-like' prowess of men and persecutes the 'sluttiness' of promiscuous women.

Being a single swinger is undoubtedly more difficult for women.

Detractors make the role more damning for women if their secret is ever exposed. And, ultimately, because our society is not particularly safe, single swinging is far more dangerous for women. However, those SBFs I spoke with believe they are in the optimum position to enjoy swinging to its full potential. Aside from being able to have their pick of who they want when they want them, they aren't saddled with a partner who might hamper their fun with limitations and conditions. Answering only to the dictates of their own libido they can play with singles or couples whenever it best suits them and, usually, on their own terms. The endless invitations are constantly being proffered and the opportunities for satisfaction seem to be never ending.

According to the figures given by swinging websites, the membership ratios show the SBF is not a myth, although she could be listed as an endangered species. Single female membership usually equates to one tenth of a site's single male membership. To state that more explicitly: for every single female listed on an internet swingers' database, there are at least ten single males advertising. On the positive side, this suggests that websites are the ideal place for couples to pick and choose if they intend to organise a MFM [Male/Female/Male] threesome. But, for those who want to negotiate a successful FMF threesome, the chances look very remote.

Which is not to say FMF threesomes don't happen. All these statistics really prove is that single women are less inclined to promote themselves through the internet. The reasons could be manifold, ranging from a distaste for internet adult personals through to an adequate supply of local males obviating the need to advertise via the net. The majority of SBFs I encountered while researching this book did not advertise online, which suggests it's not the favoured milieu for this category of swingers.

During a recent conversation with the female producer of a Channel 4 documentary on contemporary attitudes towards sex, we both agreed that women are taking a more forceful role in what has traditionally been a male-driven environment. She opined that, thanks to increased media interest in the subject of female pleasure, women are now better informed about the sexual opportunities available to them and are actively seeking personal satisfaction. The women who appear on the following pages are at the forefront of this trend as it takes place behind the doors of the swinging community.

Darla is a nineteen-year-old single mother. Tall, slim, with dark hair and dark eyes, she was introduced to swinging by an older boyfriend and then separated from him. She is openly bisexual and giggles at the idea of being described as 'between partners'.

Darla: 'I'd split up with my previous boyfriend, the one who introduced me to swinging, and I'd got with this new guy who seemed more dependable and stable. He was a lovely man but, when I told him that I wanted to carry on swinging, he freaked out and called me a slag.'

Our conversation takes place in Darla's meticulously tidy home, during the early evening. Darla speaks quickly when talking about the men and women in her life, but the speed of her words slows down when she reaches more comfortable topics. 'Generally, when a man calls me a slag, I think it's a good thing. But, from the way he said it, I could see he was suddenly scared of me. I suppose I should have seen the warning signs before that. We'd been talking about sex and I'd asked what he was into and he'd just said, "The usual stuff." I asked him what he meant by *the usual stuff* because that didn't really explain much to me. For me *the usual stuff* was having a cock in my mouth and another in my pussy, or a pussy in my mouth and some woman sucking my nipples, or a pile of naked male and female bodies on top of me, so I kind of guessed that our definitions of *the usual stuff* were going to differ. I asked him if he liked blowjobs and he shrugged and said he guessed they were OK. And I think that was when I should have realised we were sexually mismatched. He's the only man I've ever met who thinks that blowjobs are only OK. But I must have been a bit slow on the uptake, because the discovery that we were mismatched didn't hit me until I suggested swinging. That was when he got scared and called me a slag.'

She frowns, clearly disappointed that the relationship hadn't had a more satisfactory outcome. Darla has already mentioned that her ideal man is proving elusive and hard to find. Talking about her break-up looks like a minor ordeal but she bravely continues. 'It was a shame, because I'd mentioned swinging in the hope he would take me to a swingers' party. It had been a long time since I'd eaten some pussy and I was getting restless. As it was obvious he couldn't cope with the idea of swinging and swingers, I ended up going on my own.' She says the words as though her decision to go to the party alone was the point where she realised the relationship had ended.

'I've always thought that women who go to swingers' parties alone are stupid. It's a dangerous thing for a single woman to do. As much as everyone likes to think we women are totally liberated and strong enough to look after ourselves, we're not. If you get a room full of men that are looking for sex – a gang of them all with their cocks out – you've got no assurance that they're going to accept that "no" means "no". Drinks are flowing, people are going to get pissed and there are lots of places where "no" is quite a turn-on for some men. I've always thought that women who say they regularly go to parties on their own are just talking shit. I've only done it a couple of times and I only went on those occasions because I knew and trusted the people who were running the party.

'And it was because I knew and trusted the couple running *that* party that I figured I might risk going by myself. It was being held at a place I'd gone to with my previous boyfriend. Anne and Simon, the hosts, had called me to offer the invitation. And even though I didn't have anyone to go with, I said I would probably go.' She leans forward in her seat, lowers her voice and puts her mouth closer to the microphone. 'I think part of the reason I was agreeing was because I was getting desperate to fuck someone more unconventional than the man I was with. He didn't go beyond the missionary position and that was doing nothing for me. But also, as I said, I was desperate for some pussy. I'm not a man-hater. I like men as friends and sexual partners. But there are some things that a woman can do so much better than a man and that was what I needed.'

Darla explains that she hadn't officially broken up with her partner when she decided to attend the swingers' party alone but she had also known that the end of the relationship was clearly in sight. 'I know it was behind his back. And I know it was cheating. But I didn't plan to learn the names of anyone I fucked so I didn't think it was that big a deal.

'It ended up being a really good night. I was wearing my little PVC dress with buckles at the front. It was black. It wasn't that short – about mid-thigh length.' She illustrates the dress's length by drawing a line with one hand high up on her thigh. 'It wasn't that low-cut either. It was quite modest in a way but it was the tightest thing I'd ever owned and it had buckles on the front and reminded me of those sexy straitjackets.' She laughs at this and the conversation breaks off into a discussion about whether or not straitjackets can be described as 'sexy'. Aside from swingers' parties, Darla has also experimented with bondage and discipline and she argues passionately that straitjackets do have a strongly erotic appeal. 'I liked the buckles,' she says eventually, turning the topic back to the PVC dress she had worn that night. 'I liked the buckles because, as well as giving me a feeling of being restrained, it was like a sign to everyone that said, "You're not getting in here unless I say so."

'I had no knickers. High-heel shoes. No stockings. The last time I'd been to a party in fishnets they'd got caught on someone's thigh-high boots and I didn't want that to happen again.

'The party invitation was still an option but my first thoughts were to explore the gay bars and see if I could pull. Frustratingly, that night, all the bars in town were just full of rough-looking girls. The ones I was interested in either weren't interested in me, or they were in exclusive relationships and could only look without touching. I got fed up with nothing happening so I decided to take up Simon and Anne on their offer and went to their club.'

Darla pauses and sits back in her chair. She appears more relaxed now the subject has moved on to the party. Her tone of voice suggests she has a genuine appreciation of Simon and Anne's friendship. 'They were really pleased to see me when I got there but I got the idea that by paying so much attention to me they were neglecting their duties to everyone else at the party. Simon was constantly chatting to me, telling me I looked nice and bringing me drinks. Anne kept touching my leg under the table. I was enjoying their attention but eventually I felt as though I was imposing and said, "Your job is to mingle," and sent them away.' They ended up going and snorting coke in the bathroom but I figured that was their decision. I didn't need babysitting and I was certain that their job wasn't to look after me. Being fair to them, they offered me some of their coke but I said no thanks and told them, "Nothing's going up my *nose* this evening."' She laughs again, acknowledges that there were other places where she desperately wanted things to 'go up', but insists that she couldn't see the attraction in putting anything up her nose.

'When they'd gone, I wished that Anne had stayed behind. While she'd been touching my leg I'd started masturbating. It's not something I'd ever done in a busy club before – not even in a swingers' club. But my skirt was short, I was very horny, I wasn't wearing knickers and no one seemed to mind. It's quite exciting to be touching yourself in a room full of people, especially when everyone can see what you're doing. I suppose I was getting frustrated because Anne's hand had felt very good against my leg, and masturbation seemed like the most obvious outlet.

'Anne is an attractive woman. Her figure always reminds me of Roger Rabbit's wife, Jessica Rabbit. Facially, she isn't perfect. But her body is slim and curvy and, because that evening she was wearing a tight rubber dress, she looked absolutely irresistible. My previous boyfriend had said she wanted me from the day I first stepped into their club. But nothing had ever happened even though we'd been there a few times as regulars. After I'd sent her and Simon away that evening, I was instantly thinking, "Come back, Anne. I want you. I want you now."

'A handful of guys came over to talk to me but I wasn't there for men. I wanted a woman and I told them as much. I think the word must have gotten back to Anne because, when she came out from behind the bar, she was naked and wearing a big strap-on. She headed straight to my table and stood over me while I continued to masturbate. My first thoughts were directed to everyone else at the party. I was thinking, "Can you lot all go away now, please? I'm not sharing this absolutely huge thing with any of you. It's all mine."

'My pussy isn't so large that it's able to easily take a huge cock. I've been with guys with big dicks and it restricts the positions you can comfortably manage. Anne was wearing this gigantic strap-on and I was thinking that I might not be able to take it all, but I was going to have a lot of fun trying.

'She got me to suck her cock first. She's basically a very domineering woman. I suppose, when you're regularly hosting parties the way she does, you have to have a dominant nature. So she had no problems telling me to kneel on the floor and suck her cock. Simon was nearby but it looked like he'd been given instructions not to join in until she'd given him permission. I liked the fact that she had him so well trained. Anne got me to lick and suck at her cock while everyone in the bar stood on the dance floor watching.

'I continued to masturbate while I sucked her. I continued until Anne ordered me to stand up and bend over so she could fuck me from behind. I was amazed that she got so much of it inside me. I suppose I was pretty wet with excitement, and I had licked and sucked her cock so it was really well lubricated. She kept pushing her cock into me for about ten minutes, riding me as well as any man, and then she decided we should carry on in the Jacuzzi.

'The Jacuzzi was only a short way from the bar.' Darla steals my notepad and draws a diagram of the club's floor plan. 'The club is separated into a bar area, playrooms upstairs, a place downstairs with a wet room where all the pissing goes on, and a Jacuzzi at the end of the hall.' She indicates each area on the diagram as she names the rooms. 'There were a couple of other girls in the Jacuzzi but they weren't playing with anyone – as though they were just there to be part of the scenery. It was exciting to know they were watching, along with the guys that had followed us in, but I was so desperate for Anne I wanted to tell them all to fuck off and get out of my space and leave me and Anne alone to enjoy each other.

'She took her cock off before she got into the water. And then she was on me and kissing me and touching me. The difference between a man and a woman kissing, and a woman and a woman kissing, is all in their use of tongues. When a man and a woman kiss, because they can do other things, because they've got a cock and a pussy and they fit together appropriately, there's more that they can do while they're kissing. Men and women get lazy and they just kiss with their lips and it's rarely anything special. But female kissing can be far more intimate and dirty. Tongues can go everywhere. And it's rarely just a matter of putting tongues in each other's mouth. It's tongues all over your face. It's tongues along your neck. It's tongues everywhere. And you're full of this person's spit. And it's just filth. And it's great.' Darla sighs and falls silent for a moment, her gaze contemplating a faraway memory. Then, with a swift laugh and a grin, she's back in the room and again talking about the party. 'Anne had her fingers inside me while we kissed in the Jacuzzi, and I finally got the chance to slide my fingers inside her pussy. The slippery sensation of the water – Anne touching me, and so many people watching – all added to my excitement. She licked my face, throat, neck and breasts. I felt wonderful. When Anne went under the water, and started to lick me while I was still in the Jacuzzi, I thought it was the most mind-blowing thing ever.

'There were bubbles coming up from the water as she licked me. And, although the pleasure was fantastic, I was beginning to panic that she might be running out of breath or dying from lack of oxygen or something. No one who was watching seemed overly concerned about Anne, everyone seemed to be watching me as I got closer and closer to my orgasm. Eventually, I stopped worrying about Anne and her need to breathe and I relaxed into the moment.

'Just before I came, I was reading the signs on the wall around the Jacuzzi. One of them said NO PISSING. Another one was telling people to act responsibly. And there was another sign that said no one should come in the pool.

'I read that one last and just smiled and thought: *too late*.'

Eliza is twenty-eight years old, slim, bisexual, athletic and works as a lap-dancer in a Birmingham nightclub. In her spare time she also does some glamour modelling. Eliza first became involved in swinging through the invitation of a customer at the lap-dancing club where she works. She has since moved on to become a 'ticket' charging a minimum of £1,000 to escort a customer to a swingers' club while posing as his partner. Even though 'tickets' are frowned on by the swinging community, Eliza believes she provides a valuable service and offers good value for money.

Eliza: 'Not many people like the fact that I charge money. When you mix money with sex people automatically think you're a prostitute and all the usual crap starts. But, when you work in a lap-dancing bar, the regulars are always asking you to go out with them. A lot of them think, because you work as a lap-dancer, you're the ideal person to escort them to a swingers' club. And, since I'm there to earn money and not broaden my social life, I figure it makes sense to charge the punters for my time.

'I charge £1,000 to attend a party. I'll charge more if I think the punter will pay that much. Which means I get to go swinging: but I do it at someone else's expense.' She flashes a broad smile that gleams with triumph. 'I think I would probably be swinging anyway, even if people weren't paying me to go. I've done a couple of parties alone and just went for the pleasure. Swingers' parties are usually a giggle and, because I've got a fairly decent figure and I'm used to showing it off through the lap-dancing –' she pulls at the hem of her sweater as she says this, emphasising the shape of her large breasts '– I get lots of attention. Obviously, when I'm with a punter, I have to keep it quiet that I'm paid to be there. Swingers are generally nice enough people but they get pretty pissed off if they learn someone's there as a ticket. I don't know if it's because they're jealous that I'm getting paid to enjoy myself while they're having to spend money for the same result, or if it's something else. But I don't tell anyone that I'm earning from being there. And I insist that none of my punters tell anyone either.'

Our conversation takes place in a Midlands coffee shop. Eliza is drinking a tall Caffé Americano – an espresso with hot water. There is something about the efficiency and elegance of the drink that is reminiscent of Eliza and her no-nonsense approach to being paid to attend swingers' parties.

'I don't think £1,000 is an excessive amount of money. One of the girls I work with charges £5,000 and upwards to escort a punter to a swingers' party, although she does give them full value for their money. I provide good value, I think, but I don't do half the stuff she does.' With an intriguing snort of disdain she adds, 'I *wouldn't* do half the stuff she does. Usually I'll set out ground rules before we go anywhere. We may or may not have sex at the party. It depends if I'm in the mood. I may or may not have sex with other men at the party. Again, it depends if I'm in the mood. There's a strong likelihood that I will have sex with a woman at the party. I do like having sex with women, and swingers' parties usually provide the opportunity. But this depends on whether or not I meet an acceptable woman who wants to have sex with me, and also whether or not I'm in the mood.'

She sips her coffee and then raises her gaze defensively. 'It sounds harsh. The punter is paying me £1,000 and, effectively, I'm promising him nothing in return. But if he doesn't want to pay he doesn't have to pay. No one's forcing him. And I'm pretty much a party animal when I get started. I just never make rash promises.

'If he's agreeable to my conditions we'll get our stories straight. We go there and pretend to be a new couple. If anyone asks, we say we've both tried swinging before, with previous partners, but now we're together we're trying it as a couple. This explains things neatly, especially if there's anyone at the party that either of us have met before. It also means we don't get some condescending prat taking us through the rules and protocols of swinging parties as if we were newbies and wasting most of our evening.'

When asked which rules and protocols she means, Eliza rolls her eyes and wearily recites the list of conditions that most experienced hosts use when introducing newcomers to the formalities of a swingers' party. It's an extensive list and the details are familiar to both of us. She keeps her voice lowered, out of deference for the people sitting near us. Thoughtfully, she moves her mouth closer to the microphone of the cassette recorder that is capturing our conversation. 'Respect the limitations of the other partygoers. No means no and anyone ignoring that rule will be forcibly ejected. Use condoms at all times. Do not practise any dangerous activities such as choking games, bloodsports or excessive BDSM. Always stay together as a couple. No single men are allowed to wander around the party without their partner.' She pauses, frowns and then says, 'Everyone says that about single men. But I don't think I've ever been to a party where there haven't been a few single men wandering aimlessly around. Some of them are there as singles anyway. A few of them are often miserable husbands who've either lost their wives for the evening, or they've lost their erections and they're trying not to be embarrassed about the situation.' Her smile is cruel as she adds this last observation. She sips a little more of her Caffé Americano before continuing.

'I usually have fun when I go to a party. Well, when you're getting paid £1,000 to go to a party you're bound to have fun, aren't you? But I think it's more fun when I'm going on my own, without a punter paying for the company of my pleasure. Single girls are always the centre of attention at swingers' parties and it really is a kick to be so universally desired.

'If I'm with a punter we'll spend the evening together. As I said before, the hosts at swingers' parties don't like it when couples go their separate ways, and I can't imagine any of my punters would be happy if I dumped them on the doorstep with their £1,000 in my purse. We might get funky in a playroom or try to get involved with a group thing. But it depends what the punter wants from the evening and whether or not it suits my mood. Whatever it is, I'll usually try to enjoy myself.

'If I go on my own, I'll get off with a single woman or a couple and the whole evening will be a lot more intimate, private and secluded. It's possible to be private like that with a woman, even at a busy swingers' party. That sort of connection just isn't possible if you hook up with a man.

'The first time I went to a party I had no idea what to expect so I went a little OTT. I'd gone with a punter from the lap-dancing club. There was music and a pole, so I ended up doing some pretty raunchy pole-dancing. It went down well. Everyone watching applauded. Some people tried to get in on the act and there was a lot of touching but nothing I hadn't expected and no more than I could handle. It was more than I would do nowadays but it was a fun way for me to become the centre of attention. At that first party my date introduced me to a couple of guys and the four of us ended up in one of the playrooms.' Eliza's voice had risen up to a normal level but she whispers again as she explains the positions she assumed in the playroom and talks about the various ways in which she had sex with the three men. The soft sound of her tone makes the events seem as though they were intimate and powerfully erotic. 'Having three cocks pushed into me was about the limits of what I'd said I would allow. But it was a good and satisfying experience. Just because I was being paid didn't mean I couldn't get off. And, with those three guys trying to outdo each other, and with there also being some other sexy stuff going on nearby, it all worked out very well for me. I think the only thing that spoilt that first evening for me was the fact that I came close to copping off with a very sexy blonde woman and then it didn't happen.'

Eliza winces as she drinks, as though her Caffé Americano is either too hot or too cold. 'She was striking. Tall, busty and looking really hot in black stockings, heels, thong and bra. My punter had disappeared outside for a fag with his two new friends, the three of them had left me on the playroom bed after we'd all come, and she came over to me and started touching me. First there was a hand on my thigh. Then she stroked my boob and teased the nipple. And then she was kissing me full on the mouth. Her tongue pushed into me; she treated me to a kiss that was really vigorous, passionate and had me desperate to fuck her; and then she pulled away. She said, "Your breath tastes of spunk." And that was the last I saw of her that evening. Or ever.'

Eliza waves the matter away with an impatient flick of her hand. 'But aside from that, the experience was a good taster. My punter seemed happy, I'd been serviced and satisfied, and I realised I could be a ticket in future and not have to do nearly so much hard work. After that first evening I also decided to try visiting one of the parties and see if it was more fun when I wasn't there for the pleasure of a paying customer.

'As I said, when I go to a party on my own it is a different experience. I'll get a drink and mingle with couples that I find attractive, and I'll spend a lazy night getting close to the most attractive woman I can find. If I'm there with a punter

I'll try and get involved with a woman who isn't quite as attractive.' Eliza settles more comfortably into her seat, pulls her sweater tight again, and expands on this theme. 'Everyone says that they want to have sex with people who are attractive. But if a woman's ever serious about it, she doesn't want someone more attractive than her. Not when there's a man around who'll be making comparisons. If I'm with a punter I deliberately look for someone less attractive because I want to be the fittest one there. If I'm on my own, I want to be sure that I've scored with the best-looking woman in the place.

'If I ever end up in a serious relationship I'll probably give up the parties altogether. I don't think parties are the right place for a couple who want a healthy relationship. Whether I end up with a steady boyfriend or girlfriend, if I carry on going to parties – if *we* carry on going to swingers' parties – my partner's going to see people doing things to me that they won't like. Things that they can't do. Things that they're not able to do. And, if I do end up in a serious relationship, I'm not going to let anything like swinging spoil it. I've heard lots of women at parties say they got into swinging with their husbands, and then they say that they're divorced now. As the conversation carries on you learn that they've carried on swinging with the person that broke up their marriage. And I always wonder, were they really so naïve when they got into it?' She shakes her head, obviously amazed at the apparent lack of insight. 'Unless someone's absolutely secure in their relationship, unless they know one hundred and ten per cent that they won't want more than just sex from the people they meet, they shouldn't do it. I honestly believe I can fuck somebody without feeling anything for them. I can have an orgasm with a man or a woman. I can come all over some guy's cock or some woman's hand or tongue. And I'm not really bothered who they are, or what their name is, or anything about them other than that they're making me enjoy myself.

'But I can imagine all that would change if I ended up in a serious relationship. And if I have something special with someone, I don't want to spoil it with something as frivolous as swinging.' She finishes her drink and, when she glances towards the door of the coffee shop, she makes it clear that our interview is drawing to a close. Eliza lowers her voice for a final time before saying goodbye and adds, 'I'm going to carry on visiting the swinging parties until that serious relationship does come along. And I'll be going on my own as well as going every time someone pays the £1,000 for my services.'

Fiona is forty years old and bisexual. She lives in Hertfordshire with her daughter, her partner Fred, and Fred's son. Fiona has been swinging since she was eighteen. An attractive redhead, she abstained from swinging for a decade when she got married. However,
Fiona returned to the lifestyle as a single bi female which is how she met Fred.

Fiona: 'We met through SEX UK. We were both on there. Both of us were with other partners at the time. Partners who weren't giving us what we wanted sexually. That's how it all started. We were both open with each other and we met purely for sex. It turned out to be rather fantastic sex. Hence the fact that we are now both together and without our other partners.'

The conversation takes place in Fiona's kitchen on a Saturday afternoon. She's already told me that, once we've finished talking, she and Fred will be getting ready to visit their local swingers' club. 'Part of our easy acceptance of swinging was because I've swung for a long time. I was eighteen when I first got involved in it. I was with a boyfriend then and working for a thirty-five-year-old bloke who introduced me to swinging. I did it for seven years from then – up until I got married. I got married when I was twenty-five and I didn't do any swinging at all until recently when I met Fred. Swinging wasn't something that interested my husband so I simply didn't do it. He had no idea that I'd gone to SEX UK.'

Fiona's accent has the cultured tone of someone who has lived in Hertfordshire for a long time. But, when the topic shifts to her past, it's possible to detect the undercurrent of a slight Brummie drawl.

'After ten years of marriage, I'd had enough. I'd reached the stage in my life where I needed to make some huge decisions. I was weaving my way up in the civil service. Five days a week I was taking my daughter to a child minder at quarter to eight on a morning and picking her up at six o'clock at night. I used to go to London probably once a month with my job. I'd have to go up to Newcastle every month for a couple of days too. My mum was looking after my daughter as much as I was. I'd been doing that for two and a half to three years, and I suddenly thought: No! I'm not doing this any more.

'I was with a lovely guy. He'd got his own business and an absolutely beautiful, huge five-bedroom house. It was close to being perfect But I didn't love him. I fancied him but that's not enough to sustain a marriage. I used to come home so bloody frustrated. I liked him. I liked spending time with him. My daughter got on with his kids. But that's all it was. And that's all it ever would be. Just comfortable. I had to find something else. That's when I first subscribed to SEX UK. And that's where I met Fred.'

She smiles at her partner and, when she next speaks, the lilt of a Brummie drawl is gone from her accent. 'Fred had been married twice before we met. His first wife was abusive, promiscuous and quite nasty. She left him with pretty low self-esteem. He went from her to another woman who was just the opposite of his first wife – kindness, acceptance and great with his son – but she wasn't what you'd call sexually adventurous. She didn't much care for sex at all. Swinging was something that had always interested Fred but he'd never had the chance to explore that interest.

'So, because his first wife had been doing it to him for so many years, he decided it was time for him to have some extra-marital fun. His second wife worked away from home quite a lot, which left him with plenty of free time. And he registered on SEX UK where we ended up chatting for a few months.' Fred sits with us at the kitchen table, nodding agreement and glancing fondly at his partner. 'It wasn't what you'd call a whirlwind romance,' Fiona continues. 'I met up with a few couples, telling Fred about my experiences and having a laugh and a joke with him. We'd meet in the chatroom and wind each other up. It was a long time before we trusted each other enough to swap mobile numbers but, unlike a lot of the single blokes you meet online, Fred didn't put any pressure on me for my number.' She pauses for a moment and, when she next speaks, the Birmingham accent has briefly resurfaced. 'That happened just after I'd left my husband. I quit my job. I moved out of the area to live with my younger brother. And I practically started my life again. I worked part-time. I spent more time with my daughter. I was determined to start having a sex life that was satisfying and fulfilling. Which is why I agreed to meet Fred.'

The couple exchange a glance that makes it obvious they are very fond of each other. It's also obvious, if Fiona hadn't agreed to be interviewed this Saturday afternoon, they would most likely be alone in a room and preparing for their night out at the local swingers' club. This blatant connection makes one wonder how the couple are able to swing and not make those they are swinging with feel excluded by their bond. However, it's not a question worth raising because Fiona and Fred's obvious affection makes it clear that neither of them have ever considered this to be an issue. 'We met at a pub,' Fiona explains. 'We'd swapped photos online so we knew who we were looking for. And the sexual chemistry was there, between us, straight away. I'd gone there with the attitude of, "This is who I am. This is what I do. This is what I want." And I figured he would either accept me on those terms or we could have a drink and then go our separate ways. I hadn't expected we would share such a strong attraction. And our first kiss was just, "WOOF!"'

The sound of her laughter fills the kitchen after this exclamation. Fred grins supportive agreement to show that the word 'WOOF!' is the closest either of them can get to articulating that immediate connection. 'We ended up in bed together on that first date,' Fiona continues. 'We'd only gone to meet each other for sex. But it turned out to be pretty fantastic sex. We agreed to meet again and, so there was no danger of either of us thinking that it was more than just a swinging date, we arranged to meet up with another girl and have a threesome.

'I think that was when I realised that I'd found the perfect partner in Fred. The girl we were with was very young and sexy. She satisfied both of us and we made it a special night for her. My philosophy is, with another woman, we know our own bodies best. I think it's accepted that two women can pleasure each other better than a lot of men could pleasure a woman. Women understand what things feel like and men don't seem to see that in the same way. But, that evening, even though the girl we were with was good, both me and Fred got more excitement and pleasure from being with each other.

'The next date we arranged was at a swingers' club. Fred had never been to a swingers' club before. He spent the whole evening with his mouth hanging open and his jaw on his chest. They had a very big playroom with three or four double beds and a lot of the customers just used to go in there, get naked and join in together. We started off having sex with each other in the playroom but there was a threesome going on close to us. We were watching them while we were with each other – one man, his partner and their girlfriend – and we kept edging closer and closer. Eventually we were so close it was easy for us to say, "Mind if we join in?" And before the evening was over we'd started a substantial orgy. The playroom was a mass of arms and legs. All naked bodies writhing together.' Fiona laughs again and says, 'We had a whale of a time.

'And we arranged to meet again. Our dates became more and more frequent. They started off as once every couple of weeks but soon it was every week. Then it was every time Fred's wife was out of town on business. During one date we registered as a couple on Local Swingers. Then we'd organise meets with other couples. That continued until Fred finally admitted that he didn't want to be with his wife any more – he wanted to be with me.'

Fiona's Birmingham accent has disappeared. It's no longer apparent whether she's talking about her relationship with Fred for the benefit of our interview, or reminding her partner of their good fortune. 'I can't begin to describe the ways that we're suited for each other. We're both bisexual, so that makes the swinging more interesting. I enjoy watching two men together and I know that Fred likes watching two women. The bisexuality poses a few problems when we date couples. Neither of us is really looking for a straight swap. We both want some same-sex excitement if we're meeting a couple. If we want a good heterosexual experience we can get that from each other at home. But we're both honest enough to admit that, and it's the honesty that makes the swinging so much fun.'

Fiona and Fred seem so closely involved it had made me curious as to how they were able to swing without making other partners feel excluded. Now, I'm beginning to understand that neither of them are overly concerned about whether or not their other partners feel excluded. They are only swinging for the pleasure it gives them and each other.

'Swinging enhances our relationship,' Fiona explains. 'Just like somebody else going out to the pub and having a drink. We go out to the club for sex. We have a great time with other likeminded people, who are all there for exactly the same thing, and then we come home and have an absolutely fantastic time. Obviously I've got a young daughter, and Fred has his son, so it's difficult for us to get out. But if there's a month when we can't go out swinging, that's fine. It's not a problem. It's not something that we *have to do*. But it's something that we *really enjoy doing*. It keeps our relationship exciting. And, because we met knowing that's what we like to do, it's just become part of us.

'We started off with a lot in common and I think we've grown to have so much more in common. Sexually, Fred's not inhibited and knows he can suggest anything to me. And I'm not embarrassed to say anything to him. It seems as though everything we try together is enjoyable. The only thing that we're now slightly wary of are single women. Some of them out there aren't just looking for a bi-experience. Some of them are looking for a bloke.' She laughs without humour and says firmly, 'They're not having mine.'

FUN AND FRIENDSHIP

> **Couple Seeks Couple for** adult fun and
> friendship. Cleanliness and discretion
> expected and assured. P.O. Box AL003

Logically and rationally, it shouldn't shock any of us when friends have sex with friends. Few people express surprise if platonic colleagues fraternise outside office hours. Friends holiday with friends. Friends watch films together and friends share meals and drinks and conversations. Most individuals and communities encourage socialisation, bonding and general camaraderie. But, when those friendships become sexual relationships, particularly if they are uncommitted and casual sexual relationships, the response is usually shock and outrage.

At first glance, it's hard to explain the reasoning behind this reaction. If anyone, male or female, admits to a one-night stand, few people express surprise. Sex with strangers is not specifically condoned but it's no longer considered irredeemably deviant behaviour. However, if two friends confess that they had sex, the typical reaction is often disbelief, incredulity and even condemnation.

Admittedly, there are a growing number of friends who

term themselves *fuck buddies*. These relationships combine platonic friendships with casual sex to serve the purpose of 'scratching a mutual itch'. But, even though this contemporary arrangement does incorporate an element of in-yer-face bravado, it's usually a private endeavour and the details are very rarely discussed outside those involved.

The taboo on having sex with friends was a subject that was repeatedly mentioned during interviews with swingers for this book. One astute lady from Newcastle pointed out that if all four of her neighbours, the Smiths and the Joneses, were involved in illicit extra-marital affairs, the situation would be considered immoral, but otherwise unremarkable. Mr Smith might be deemed a philanderer; Mr Jones would be lauded for being 'one of the lads'. Mrs Smith and Mrs Jones would likely be labelled as nymphomaniacs by anyone aware of their respective secrets although, if one of the women were involved with a younger man, she would be quietly envied for having a toyboy. However, if the Smiths and the Joneses were good friends who met each weekend for a fourway – all of them consenting and none of them doing anything without their partner's knowledge or approval – they would be considered amongst the planet's most subversive and reprehensible deviants.

Despite the negative associations that society inflicts on this situation, friends continue to have sex with friends. The interviews on the following pages focused on this sensitive subject and addressed some of the problems that are faced by swinging with friends.

Gloria and Gordon have been married for twelve years and swinging for five. They live in Glasgow and Gloria works part-time in administration for a local solicitor. Her husband, Gordon, is a butcher. Thirty-six and thirty-eight respectively, Gloria has one child from a previous marriage. They were introduced to swinging by their close friends and neighbours Jack and Linda.

Gloria: 'We'd known Jack and Linda for about five years when it started. We'd known them from the day we moved into this house. We were neighbours, we were all a similar age, and we just seemed to get along together.' Gloria glances towards the wall that links their house to the neighbouring semi. She has taken the afternoon off work for our interview and is still dressed in a smart office suit. Her conservative appearance is a stark contrast to the photographs she has shown revealing a semi-naked Gloria in the throes of passion with a variety of men and women. 'Throughout the week Jack and Gordon would go to the pub at the end of the day. Linda would pop round to me and we'd chat about work, TV and general stuff. In the summer we'd have barbecues together, sunbathe in each other's gardens and forever be in and out of each other's houses borrowing food or drink or lending clothes or videos. Linda was always my first choice when I was looking for a babysitter. Jack and Gordon would spend hours working on each other's cars or doing the odd two-man job at one of our houses. We were close. At the time I thought we were as close as friends could get. I didn't think it was possible for us to get closer.

'I suppose I did wonder what Jack and Linda got up to on their weekends. Three weekends out of four they'd be away and we'd be keeping an eye on their house. They never said where they were going and, because we were all good friends – best friends – I didn't like to intrude and I never thought to ask.' Gloria blushes a little, giving the impression that she might have raised the question but never received a satisfactory answer. When she later admits that Jack and

Linda had been new to swinging when they first became neighbours, and had been trying to keep their lifestyle secret from non-swinging friends, it sounds as though Gloria is still a little upset by their lack of trust. 'It was usually just a case of Linda popping round to say they were off, asking if I could feed the tropical fish or water the houseplants, and then we wouldn't see them again until we were all back home from work on the Monday evening. But neither Gordon nor I asked, and neither Jack nor Linda offered the information, so we spent five years building up a good, solid friendship and being oblivious to the fact that they were swingers. We only found out about their swinging, five years into our friendship, after we'd had a Monday evening meal together. Gordon had picked up some extra steaks from his shop and we thought it would be pleasant to invite Jack and Linda round for their tea. It was nothing out of the ordinary. I think we did it more Monday nights than not. My lass, Laura, was spending the night at a friend's so there were only us adults in the house. We'd just finished eating, Linda and I had stacked the dishwasher, and Jack and Gordon were in the kitchen, raiding the fridge for beers.

'I asked, "Does anyone fancy a game of cards?"

'Linda said, "As long as it's not strip poker. I lost a pair of my best Anne Summers knickers last week playing that fucking game."

'It was one of those comments that they describe as "a bombshell". Jack was staring incredulously at Linda. Gordon looked mystified. And I don't think Linda realised what she'd said. When she saw we were all staring at her – gaping at her – she turned bright red. The expression on her face looked like she was thinking, *Did I say that out loud?*

'"You lost a pair of knickers playing strip poker?" I repeated. "Are you going to tell us the rest of that story? Or do we have to use our imagination to fill in the blanks?"

'Linda and Jack exchanged a glance. It looked like she was asking him if it was OK to tell us. He shrugged, as if he was saying it was her decision. Linda gave this big heavy sigh and then said, "You'd best grab a drink to hear this one." Then she took Jack's tin of lager and announced that they'd been swinging since they got married. They usually saw other couples, although they'd started to prefer the atmosphere of clubs and parties over the past few years, hence the long weekends away. When Gordon and I both looked puzzled she said, in simple terms, they met up with strangers and had sex with them.'

Gloria chuckles, recalling the surprise of that evening. 'I don't know about Gordon, but I do know that I was pretty shocked. We made out like it was nothing out of the ordinary, and continued the rest of the evening as normal. But, once they'd left, it was the first thing Gordon and I talked about. He asked, "Are you OK with our neighbours having sex with strangers?"

'I wanted to say, I'm just disappointed they haven't told us about it before. I'm sure that's what I intended to say. But, instead, I said, "I'm just upset they haven't invited us to join them." It was one of those comments that led to a very sexy evening. Possibly the sexiest evening of our marriage up to then. Our sex life had always been OK, but it had never been anything spectacular. Neither of us was into hanging from chandeliers, or jumping off the top of the wardrobe, or anything out of the ordinary, but it was always pleasant and usually satisfactory. But, that night, we both seemed far more passionate than usual.' Gloria blushes again. Like many swingers she is comfortable talking about sexual events at parties, clubs and private swaps. But when she is recounting loving intimacy with her partner the conversation is tackled as a more delicate subject. 'Afterwards Gordon asked if I'd been serious about Jack and

Linda inviting us to join them. I admitted the idea was exciting, but I wanted to find out more about it before I made a decision. Of course we'd heard about swinging and swingers' parties but we didn't really know anything about the subject. The whole idea seemed somehow forbidden, taboo, erotic and mysterious. Having Jack and Linda as neighbours and friends seemed like the ideal way to find out more but it also seemed unreal to talk to our friends about having sex with other people.

'I don't think I'd looked at Jack before as being a potential sex partner. I thought of him as Linda's husband and Gordon's friend. He was reasonably attractive, funny and amicable, but I'd never thought, *I wonder what it's like having sex with him*. And I'd certainly never looked at Linda in that way.

'But, over the course of the following week, I started to look at a lot of things differently. Jack and Gordon went round to the pub the following night. Linda was round at mine, as usual, and I ended up asking her so many questions, about what she did, where she did it, and who she did it with, that she must have thought I was obsessive. She explained that they visited parties, met other couples and the occasional single, and hooked up for full swaps, usually in the same room. Then she explained to me what all those things meant.

'I asked all the usual questions. The important questions. The questions that seem so ridiculous now, in retrospect. What do you do if someone's repulsive? What do you do if you're not in the mood? Don't either of you get jealous? Would anyone mind that I'd still not lost all of my *mummy tummy*? What happens if you want to, but they can't or won't?

'Linda answered most of my questions but she ended up laughing at me. She said that Gordon and I should talk it over, find out if we were both interested and, if we were, she and Jack would take us to a party. It didn't surprise me to find out that Gordon had been given the same advice from Jack while the pair of them had been at the pub.

'So we talked about it, and decided that our sex life was OK but it could be better. The jealousy issues seemed like a small consideration, especially with the way Jack and Linda talked about jealousy as being a possessive and ugly trait, so we figured we would give it a try. Which is how Gordon and I ended up at our first party.'

Gloria sits back and suggests we break for coffee. She has been talking continually since the interview began. Relating how she and Gordon first got into swinging has left her looking a little dazed. She mentions that it might have been helpful if Jack and Linda had been able to meet up with us: 'Jack has lots of stories he could tell you,' she laughs. But, when she's reminded that the remit of the book is to interview female swingers only, she nods and says, 'Then it's best Linda's not here. She can be pretty tight-lipped. Unless you're a very close friend or she knows you're a swinger I don't think you'd get two words out of her on the subject.' And then we're back in Gloria's lounge, sipping our mugs of coffee and Gloria is talking about her first experience of attending a swingers' club.

'I'd like to say it was like nothing we'd expected. But, having had Jack and Linda telling us what to expect, it was exactly what we'd expected. The place was done out like a regular bar, only without alcohol. There was disco lighting over a dance floor at one end of the room. And, aside from the fact that all the women seemed to be wearing very revealing clothes, it was pretty much like most other clubs and bars. Admittedly there were bedrooms that were being used as playrooms, upstairs. And there was a big-screen TV playing some pretty raunchy porn. But other than that it wasn't anything special or out of the ordinary.

'At one of the tables near the bar there was a couple kissing and touching each other, more boldly than you'd probably see in most places. He had his hand up her skirt. She had one breast out and was holding his cock, wanking him, while they kissed.' No longer blushing, Gloria admits that she didn't know whether the couple wanted people to watch or not. Consequently, she and Gordon kept glancing at the pair then hurriedly looking away.

'Jack and Linda stayed with us for a while, then a couple they'd met before came in and started chatting with them and they took off and left us alone. We watched them chatting at the bar. The wife was kissing Jack very passionately. Linda was touching the husband's crotch through his trousers and giggling like a schoolgirl. A few people did come to our table and tried to chat with us, but Gordon and I were both so scared that we didn't even try to make an impression on anyone.

'Jack and Linda eventually disappeared upstairs with their husband-and-wife friends, and Gordon and I looked at each other and I asked, "Is this really our sort of thing?"

'He said, "If you're not comfortable, we can always leave."

'And, although I thought about it, I didn't want to leave.

'Jack and Linda had made their adventures sound really exciting and I wanted to see what I was missing. Their explanations and information had been so intimate it seemed to have strengthened our friendship and I didn't want to spoil what we had because I was prudish, or shy, or unsure of myself.' She blushes again and adds, 'Also, we'd spent the last week having some very passionate sex fuelled by the prospect of this evening and I didn't want to think that had all been a silly fantasy. I knew, if we just walked away from the club, our sex life was going to return to being just OK and our friendship with Linda and Jack was going to suffer.

'So, I asked Gordon, "Why don't we just go for it?" I nodded at the couple who were still sitting at the nearby table. I'd seen that his hand was up her skirt when we entered the club. Things had moved on from there and her skirt had been lifted higher. Now I could see that he'd got a couple of his fingers inside her and he was rubbing them back and forth. It wasn't half as strong as the things that were happening on the big-screen TV. But because it was so close to us; because it was the first time I'd been in the same room with another couple while they were touching each other like that; because you could smell their sex, it was far more exciting.' Gloria finishes her coffee and the cup only rattles slightly as she places into the saucer. 'Gordon and I got down to kissing and touching. It felt a little contrived at first, as though we were doing it to show off or get people's attention, rather than doing it for our own pleasure. And then, once the initial excitement started to kick in; once he touched my thigh with one hand and teased my nipple with the other; once I realised we were in a swingers' bar, and were kissing and touching: I found myself immersed in the experience. Gordon got one hand under my skirt and had his fingers against my crotch. I had his cock in my hand, and we were acting as though we were teenagers and oblivious to anyone who might be watching in the room. We must have been slightly oblivious because neither of us noticed Jack and Linda coming back. I wasn't even aware of them until Jack started laughing and said, "I see you two started without us."

'They were both sitting at our table. Gordon had undone my top and Jack could see my breasts. I'd unzipped Gordon's trousers and Linda could see his cock. And all my ideas of embarrassment, and propriety I suppose you'd call it, went out of the window. My mouth was wet from Gordon's kisses. I was sitting opposite him in a state of near-nakedness and obvious arousal. And I said, "Well, we started without you, but now you're here maybe you can both finish us off."

'Jack and Linda took us upstairs to one of the playrooms. I had sex with Jack. And Gordon had sex with Linda. Then the four of us ended up writhing together on the bed with me and Linda licking and sucking on their cocks until I didn't know whether I was pleasuring my husband or hers. The entire evening was charged with erotic passion and I can't remember how many times I orgasmed.

'I think the whole evening was what they call *a turning point*. Jack and Linda corrected us on a couple of pieces of protocol afterwards. They explained that it was only show-offs that got so involved in the main club area but they also explained that few people ever minded. Like I said before, they were our closest and best friends before we started swinging with them. And now we're closer than I ever thought it was possible to be.'

Helen is twenty-nine years old and currently single. She works as a teaching assistant at a primary school in Plymouth and took an interest in swinging two years ago while she was with her partner, Harry.

Helen: 'The stupid thing was, we didn't go into it lightly. We talked about sex and what we liked and disliked and what we wanted and what we didn't want. We explored the fantasy of having sex with other people. And then we talked about it rationally and sensibly. We made lists. We weighed up all the pros and cons and figured it would be OK if we approached it with a light-hearted attitude and didn't take the whole thing too seriously. I was worried that one of us might get jealous but I figured we were both mature enough to overcome that. I was also worried that Harry might think less of me if he saw me having sex for fun rather than as an expression of my love for him, but he assured me that he wasn't going to think less of me.' She pauses, scowls and quietly calls Harry a bastard before continuing. Her expression is pleasant and attractive, except when she's scowling. Each time she mentions his name it's obvious from her frown that her break-up from Harry still causes upset.

'So we talked about it some more before finally agreeing to do anything. I'd always wanted to do it with a woman. I suppose it's a common enough fantasy for most women. And Harry had no objection to me doing that. I guess that's a pretty big understatement. Whenever we talked about it I know that the thought of me getting nasty with a woman always got him hard and horny. He'd always wanted to have two women in the bed, so our fantasies were quite compatible. I think I've always been a little bit attracted to girls but I've never had the chance to explore my interest. Swinging seemed like the ideal way to explore my bisexual side and fulfil Harry's fantasy in one fell swoop.' Helen releases a melancholy sigh and says, 'Everything should have been OK. But the stupid thing we did was to start off having sex with a friend. I'd told Carla what we were planning. But I'd sworn her to secrecy. They say besties are supposed to tell each other everything, and I was stupid enough to believe that. Carla was really supportive about what we were planning. She said it would be good for me to explore that side of my sexuality and she thought it would be exciting for Harry too. She said she'd once nearly had sex with a girlfriend and it had been a mind-blowing experience. When I asked her what had happened she said it had been years earlier, while she was on a school trip to France. She and this other girl had been drunk or bored or both and had ended up touching each other. Carla said it hadn't gone much further than kissing and putting her fingers inside the other girl's knickers, but she still thought it was one of the hottest experiences she'd ever enjoyed.

'And, while she was telling me, I was getting fairly wet. I don't know if it was because she was talking about a really arousing situation, or if it was because she was talking about something that I desperately wanted. But I do know that talking with Carla about what I wanted to do was just as horny as talking to Harry about the same thing.

'She described it in vivid detail. She was talking about how warm it was inside this girl's knickers. How her pubes were dead scratchy against her fingers. How she went from touching warm moist knickers, to then touching short wiry hairs, and touching soft wet flesh. I have to admit, I could have rubbed myself off listening to her anecdote. Instead, I sat there, wriggling in my chair, pretending it was just a normal conversation and growing more and more convinced that we had to find a single bi female.

'I was still aware that things might not work out the way I was hoping. But I felt confident we'd planned things properly and weren't walking into things like a pair of silly, horny kids.

'Basically, we'd agreed we wanted to try having another woman in the bedroom. The idea was that she'd be bi, and the three of us would spend a night screwing.' Helen's expression is bitter as she explains, 'Harry and me would talk about it while we were making love. He'd guide me through the scenario, talking me through the idea of him kissing another woman while I watched, asking me how badly I wanted to lick a woman's pussy while he watched, and basically making our good sex great as we imagined all the things we could do. There were a few regular scenes in there. He'd say how great it would be to have two women licking his cock. I'd say how good it was going to be to lick the taste of another woman off his erection. We talked about him sliding his cock into a woman while I licked her. It was good, healthy, dirty talk that was one half fantasy and one half plan. And it was one hundred per cent arousing.

'One night, before we'd made any definite arrangements, I told Harry I was really looking forward to our swinging because of all the things Carla had said about her time with another girl. He asked me what I meant and, when he found out I'd been talking to her about our plans, he went off on one. He said I wasn't showing much discretion, talking about it before we'd even started, and he said he didn't think Carla was trustworthy enough to keep her mouth shut.

'The argument turned into a harsh one. I reminded him he'd been asking his brother for advice on the same subject. Harry said his brother wasn't a blabbermouth like Carla. We ended up shouting and bawling at each other and Harry spent the night on the couch. I suppose the argument hurt worse because part of me knew he might be right. Carla is a bit of a gossip. But I refused to see that at the time. When me and Harry finally kissed and made up I apologised for being indiscreet but I insisted he was wrong about Carla. He said we were both at fault and I assumed the argument was all over and done with. But the next time Harry saw Carla, she was round at ours, he had to go and say, "I hear Helen's been sharing the details of our sex life with you."

'Carla laughed it off and said she'd heard we were thinking about a threeway. And then, because Harry kept making comments about it, she said, "But I don't think you'll be able to satisfy two women on your own."

'The conversation kept coming back to the same subject. Harry said he'd got no idea that Carla was a dyke. Carla asked if Harry needed someone else in the bedroom because he was having erectile problems. Eventually, inevitably I suppose you'd say, the three of us ended up naked and fucking.

'The main thing I remember about that evening is that it wasn't anything like the way Harry and me had fantasised. I suppose part of that was because Carla and Harry had practically dared each other to go so far. They were goading each other, bickering and posturing, so that the atmosphere was more antagonistic than erotic.' Helen stares at the tape recorder in silence for a moment before continuing. 'I'd thought me and Harry would have been the ones who were closer when we had a threeway. It's difficult to describe, and I guess it's only a small thing, but I'd thought we would be the ones working together, pleasuring the other woman, and being pleasured by her. That way, I'd thought, me and Harry would be able to remain spiritually intimate with each other while we were physically intimate with someone else. But, as it turned out, because the other woman was Carla, she and I seemed closer, as though we were girl-friends and working together on Harry.

'We kissed while Harry watched and wanked. And even though everything went horribly wrong afterwards, I do think that first kiss with another woman was one of the most erotic experiences I've ever enjoyed. Carla had her tongue in my mouth, she touched my face, and then she started to undress me. I had no idea she could be such a sexually exciting person but she certainly got me hot and bothered. She sucked my nipples. We did a lot more kissing. And when she eventually slipped two fingers against my pussy, I was so wet they just pushed inside.

'Carla fingered me to climax, kissing me all the time and telling me I looked horny and sexy. Harry watched in amazement with his cock in his hand. Then I got to taste Carla's pussy.

'I'm not sure if I want to go with another woman again, not after what happened. But I do know that licking her was the best part of the whole experience. She tasted quite sweet, a little bit sweaty, but not unpleasant. The sensation of slipping my tongue against her labia, knowing I was finally licking another woman, got me very, very wet.

'While I was licking Carla, she took hold of Harry's cock and started to suck him. She did it really noisily, talking all the time, telling him his cock was gorgeous and tasty and saying she wanted to swallow the whole contents of his balls. She sucked him until he was ready to come and, when he warned her and said he couldn't hold it back any longer, she just kept his cock in her mouth and carried on sucking him. When he came, I could hear the slurping sound of her swallowing.

'Strangely, I didn't feel any jealousy. I didn't feel jealous throughout the evening. Another woman was sucking my boyfriend's cock but I didn't feel any of the upset that I'd worried might present a problem. I was just getting hornier and wetter. I made Carla come by licking her and fingering her.

'Harry was still watching us and, once Carla had recovered, we made his fantasy come true by both of us licking him until he was hard again. Then we took it in turns to ride up and down his cock until he'd come again. It was a very erotic, very exciting night. If it had happened with anyone else – anyone other than Carla – it would probably have converted me to swinging there and then. At the time I thought it was exactly what I wanted and me and Harry made plans to organise something similar with someone else as soon as we could.' Helen pauses. She closes her mouth. She looks like she wants to end the interview. When asked if she's OK Helen nods tersely and speaks very quickly. 'Before we could organise anything, I discovered that Harry had started seeing Carla behind my back. Why did it hurt? I suppose it was because he was cheating. When I'd been in the room, and the three of us had been playing together, it hadn't been cheating. Even if he'd been seeing her, and then telling me about it afterwards, it wouldn't have been cheating. But when I learnt that he was meeting up with her on a regular basis, and keeping it secret from me, I felt as though he'd violated my trust.'

There's another long pause. Helen fumbles through her purse and retrieves a tissue but doesn't use it.

'So Harry and me split up,' she says eventually. 'I refused to talk to Carla from then on and I haven't spoken to her since. The last I heard was that they were still fuck buddies, although Harry now has another steady girlfriend.

'All of which means, I might try swinging again one day, but it would have to be with someone I either trusted a lot, or someone who I didn't really care about, so I could treat them as badly as Harry and Carla treated me. I think it would have worked for me and Harry if he hadn't been such a cheating shit. But because he wanted to have me, the swinging and secret *tête-à-têtes* with Carla, it didn't happen.' She exercises a watery smile. 'I'd like to say it would have been a different story if we'd started swinging with someone who wasn't a friend. But I suppose, if Harry was going to cheat on me with my best friend, he'd have cheated on me with anyone else who fancied him. And, because she fucked Harry behind my back, I don't suppose Carla was that much of a friend to begin with.'

Isobel is a fifty-year-old solicitor from London whose work focuses on family law and divorce. Her current partner, Iain, has lived with her for the six years she has been swinging. Isobel turned to swinging after the end of her second marriage but she began with the insistence that all the swinging she and Iain enjoyed would remain a purely physical experience – unencumbered by any friendships.

Isobel: 'It was one of the things I stated when I first started swinging. I said, "I'll fuck men. But I don't want to become friends with them." It's ironic really because, since becoming a swinger, I now have more friends than I ever had before. And the vast majority of them are people I met through the lifestyle. The first couple we went with didn't have any problems with us not wanting to be their friends.' The interview with Isobel takes place in a pub. She kindly agreed to meet and we'd exchanged photographs before getting together so we knew what each other looked like. Isobel's pictures show a larger-than-life lady who looks aptly described by her own word 'buxom'. But the photographs have not flattered her. In person she is a very attractive lady and draws lots of attention from other customers in the pub. Isobel seems fairly comfortable with the interest she is generating.

'The swinging came about because I was discussing a divorce case with Iain where swinging had split up the clients,' she explains. 'We were talking about the various elements of the case, ended up talking about open marriages and extra-marital relationships, and before either of us properly realised it, we were discussing the excitement that must be involved with having sex with other people.

'Returning to that conversation, usually as a precursor to sex, lasted for about a month before Iain suggested looking at some swingers' websites. While we were looking at the sites, we both came across a couple who sounded like they wanted the same thing as us and we said, "Why the hell not?" But, because I knew that swinging could destroy relationships, I approached the whole subject very warily.'

She grunts with good humour and says, 'We talked the subject to death and I repeatedly insisted that we weren't going to become friends with anyone that we fucked. Iain suggested we should organise a full swap, but in separate rooms.'

Isobel explains that this style of swinging suited her perfectly. Although she knows many men find her size attractive she is self-conscious about her weight and uneasy with the idea of anyone watching her while she is naked or having sex. Separate-room swinging offered the opportunity of being able to swing without the embarrassment of being judged on her appearance. 'I was anxious to experience having sex with a variety of other men. That was the thing that appealed to me most about swinging. Obviously I wanted Iain to have the same sort of fun with other women. It wouldn't have been fair to be any other way about it. But I've got no interest in having sex with a woman, and I didn't want anyone watching. So I concurred that separate rooms would probably be the best method for us.

'We arranged the meeting over the internet. They were a couple not too far outside our age group and local enough to be practicable. They wanted separate-room swaps too and we met them at a motorway service station. The motorway service station had a motel attached and, once we'd decided we were all compatible, we booked two rooms at the motel and spent the night with other partners.' She sips her drink and pauses when asked what happened behind the closed doors of her motel bedroom. For a long moment it doesn't look like she's going to answer. 'It was very good sex,' she admits eventually. 'Very satisfying. It's hard to describe in some ways. The man I was with wasn't better at sex than Iain, or any of my other partners. But we were only there for sex. We were only using each other for sex. There was no emotional connection. It was only physical. And that was what made it exciting.' She sips her drink again to show that she has said as much as she's going to about what happened behind that closed door.

'I can't say that it improved what I already had with Iain. The sex between us had always been good. The swinging just happened as a way to enhance something that was already enjoyable. The reason we've continued swinging is because I still find it enjoyable. Very enjoyable. And, after that first encounter, I was still certain that I didn't want to become friends with any of the swingers I fucked.

'I got the impression that my aloofness wasn't as fully appreciated by some of the other couples we met. When we were introducing ourselves, whenever the conversation veered towards small talk, I'd suggest it was time to pair off and we'd all go off to our respective rooms. And the swinging progressed pleasantly like that for the first few times. We'd see most couples once – twice if they were up for it, and very occasionally three times if we'd had a lot of fun – and then we'd move on to another couple.

'And then we met up with Robert and Kelly. The sex was good the first time we met them. It was even better the second time. They suggested a third meet and I was OK with the idea but the date they suggested fell at the wrong time of the month for me.

'Robert said, "We can all meet up for a meal and a chat. We don't have to have sex. We can just have a laugh together." I was still hesitant. Iain said he'd stand behind whatever decision I made but it was clear that he had no problems going out with Robert and Kelly for a non-sexual evening.' Isobel shakes her head and releases a self-deprecatory laugh. 'It sounds foolish in retrospect. I was OK meeting strangers for sex. But I was wary about meeting people I'd had sex with for a sociable meal. I genuinely did want to meet up with Robert and Kelly again. Robert took his time over foreplay and he had a very big cock and a lot of stamina. So, although I knew it was the start of a dangerous slope towards friendship, I agreed.

'It was a good night. I suppose it was surreal to be sitting in a restaurant with two men that I had slept with, and another woman who had also slept with both those men. I kept thinking about that and getting an erotic tingle. We were able to talk openly about sex. We laughed. And we arranged to meet them again when it wasn't going to be the wrong time of the month for me.

'This meant we were going to see the couple for a fourth time. Most significantly, we invited them to ours for that next meeting. The strange thing about that meeting was that it was more exciting than any of the others. Even the first one when we hadn't known what to expect or how we would react. When we'd gone to a motorway service station or a local hotel, we'd both known we would end up having sex. That was exciting. Very exciting. But there were few doubts about how the evening would transpire. Yet with Robert and Kelly coming round to our house, our home, and because the last time we'd seen them had been strictly conversation, we didn't know if the evening would be another social event, or something sexual.' Isobel pauses and finishes her drink. We order refills before she continues. 'As it turned out, it included elements of both those things. We started off having a meal, and again the conversation was sexual, interesting, exciting and fun. Before we knew it the night was half over and, although I was anxious to have sex with Robert, I also wanted to continue chatting with him, Kelly and Iain. I think it was when Kelly and Iain started kissing, and then getting a little bit more intimate – her taking her top off and letting him suck her nipples – when I asked Robert if we should go upstairs.

'It was another night of fun, satisfying, gratuitous sex. But it was made different because we arranged to meet up with them again. I did think about calling and cancelling that fifth meeting. We'd never seen a couple so many times and both Iain and I acknowledged that we were no longer meeting up just for sex – we liked the company of Robert and Kelly. But it seemed ridiculous to have gotten into swinging because it was something we liked doing, and then to stop seeing these people because we liked them, so we met them again. And again. And again.

'We still saw other couples in between our meetings with Robert and Kelly. And I still tried to remain as aloof as possible with other couples. I always kept the sex to separate rooms and tried to keep the small talk to a minimum. But I began to think of those other swinging meets as less satisfying than the ones we were having with Robert and Kelly.

'Robert and Kelly introduced us to a few couples, insisting we'd get on like a house on fire, and were usually proved right. But I suppose it wasn't until we were round at Kelly's birthday party that I realised we had started to make a lot of friends in the swinging community. The party was made up of some of their family and some of their swinging friends, and Iain and I knew several of the couples that were there. Because they had family present we all knew that nothing sexual was going to happen at their home. But that didn't stop any of us from swapping phone numbers, introducing couples to other couples who hadn't met up before, and generally having one of the best nights a party of swingers can have without actually doing any swinging.'

Isobel admits that she is still only happy with separate-room swinging, and doubts her attitude towards that nuance will ever change, although she concedes it's possible that anything might happen, especially where swinging is concerned. 'Maybe one day I'll regret making friends with these people,' she allows. 'I've seen the way this lifestyle can lead to marriage break-ups and a lot of unhappiness. But I sincerely believe, as long as Iain and I are honest with each other, we can carry on swinging and carry on having swingers as our friends.'

WIFE WATCHING

During the research for *Swingers: True Confessions from Today's Swinging Scene*, I spoke with several proudly cuckolded husbands and they were articulate and honest in expressing the sexual arousal they achieved from seeing their partners satisfied by other men. I've since written a fiction title based on the theme of cuckoldry, as well as articles about its appeal amongst a growing number of men in today's society. And, repeatedly, I keep seeing these themes of watching and being watched.

Exhibitionism should be the perfect partner for voyeurism, but it has to be noted that not all voyeurs want to watch exhibitionists. Exhibitionism, through its inherent need to be observed, can often be perceived as unattractive because of its blatancy. Many voyeurs prefer to catch a glimpse of things that are less artificially presented – things that might otherwise have been hidden from their view. Few of the women I interviewed for this book would describe themselves as complete exhibitionists. Rather than being involved in the symbiotic relationship of a voyeur and exhibitionist, most are content to be involved with a more intimate pairing where being watched is incidental to their experience.

But the intention to watch, and the desire to be watched, comprises one of the main motives for couples becoming swingers. For a lot of couples, their involvement with swinging begins with one partner explicitly saying the words 'I'd like to see . . .' These statements, usually delivered during the sharing or confession of fantasies, typically include: 'I'd like to see you with a woman,' or 'I'd like to see you with another man,' or 'I'd like to see you getting gangbanged.' The object of these sentences varies to some degree, but it's invariably motivated by the speaker's desire to become a voyeur. The following interviews feature women involved with men who wanted to watch. Each couple's sex life has been expanded by one partner saying, 'I'd like to see . . .'

Joyce and Jason are forty-three and forty-eight respectively. Joyce is an athletic brunette with a trim figure. The couple live in South Wales where Jason is an accountant and Joyce is a part-time administrator. Joyce insists that they are not swingers. They have been married for more than twenty-two years and use the internet, digital photography and occasional outdoor trysts to satisfy their shared passion for Joyce's exhibitionism and Jason's voyeurism. Joyce also enjoys having men masturbate to climax over her naked body.

Joyce: 'Jason wanted to see me with another man before we got married. I should have noticed the signs because they were always there. It was just something I didn't think about until a long time afterwards. Because he never said anything about it, it never happened back then. But, looking back, I'm sure the idea was in his mind from very early on in our relationship.' She says this with the exasperation of a woman who has lived with her man long enough to learn all of his shortcomings. Her patient attitude implies she now knows her husband's foibles and has learnt to accept them.

'Even while we were courting he often brought a mate with him on our dates. I didn't think it was unusual at first. If we were going to the flicks he'd say, "Oh! Barry wanted to see this movie, and said he'd come with us." Or, if we were going bowling it would be, "Terry is excellent at bowling, you should see how he gets strike after strike." Or, if we were going for a meal at one of the local caffs he would say, "Gary knows the owner. If he comes with us we'll get better service and a discount on the price."

'I didn't mind having his friends with us. We come from a small village and everybody knows everybody else. So I'd have a date with my boyfriend and his mate would be sat close by, occasionally participating in the idle chitchat, but otherwise keeping himself to himself. And I never thought they were there because Jason wanted something to happen.

'If we were going out Jason would give me a call and suggest I wear a low top or a short skirt. He was always very appreciative of my figure and liked me to "show off the goods", as he called it. And even though I'd know at the back of my mind we wouldn't be alone when we went on our date, I'd do as he asked and put on a plunge top or a short skirt. Ra-ras were popular at the time and I had a couple of those that Jason liked to see me in. Then we'd go off on our date, with his mate in tow, and we'd enjoy ourselves like a typical teenage couple.

'And one of his friends would always be lurking in the background.

'If we went bowling, I'd find myself sitting next to Terry while Jason took his turn on the lane. And I'd find Terry edging closer to me, admiring my legs and my boobs, and generally flirting while Jason was away. The same thing would happen in the caff, with Jason disappearing to the loo a few times during the meal, and me being left alone with Gary or whoever else Jason had invited to join us. At the pictures, because it was dark, Jason and I would have a teenage fumble together. He'd have a hand up my skirt, or he'd open my blouse and get one of my boobs out, and all the time I'd be conscious that Barry or someone was sitting on my other side, able to see exactly what we were doing and probably able to see a lot more of my body than was decent.

'Looking back on those days I'm surprised something didn't happen then. If we went out for a drive, hoping to park somewhere, we always ended up "bumping into" one of his mates who had "surprise, surprise" picked that same location. The mate would either be there on his own or with a girlfriend. If we went out driving to find a country pub, it wasn't unheard of to find one of his mates sitting at the bar when we walked in.

'But I don't think Jason was consciously planning anything. We lived in a small village so you could never walk more than ten yards without seeing someone you knew. It was just what we were used to.

'I suppose we came close to having a threesome during those days. In the pictures, when Jason had one of my boobs out and we were kissing, I'd felt Barry's hand on my leg a couple of times. I'd once seen he was sporting a huge erection and tugging himself while he watched us. I didn't tell Jason about that, I didn't want to spoil his friendship with Barry and I'd been quite flattered that he found me so arousing. But I didn't think Jason would want me to do anything with Barry so I never suggested we take things any further and Jason never said that was what he wanted.

'We stayed faithful to each other throughout our courtship.

'We got married in eighty-five, the same day I turned twenty-one, and I was probably four months pregnant with our first. And then we spent the next few years bringing up the babies. Sex remained enjoyable. But it was always just us. Jason did bring home mates regularly from work or the pub but, like when we were courting, it never amounted to anything. Nothing sexual.' Joyce is so adamant about this it's almost tempting to think she is concealing the truth. But she insists her vehemence comes from an honest desire not to be misunderstood. She was never unfaithful to Jason before they married and never did anything with any other man.

'That sort of thing didn't start until Jason got his first digital camera,' she explains. 'Even then it was only pictures of me in a bikini, pictures of me modelling underwear, and a few pictures of me either topless or naked, but covering everything up with my hands or a towel. We always had great sex after he'd taken the pictures – it aroused us both – and I wanted to be more daring but I never dared suggest anything.

'It was Jason who asked if he could show some of the pictures to one of his friends at work. I told him no in the first place. I didn't want my naked body being shown to all and sundry. And he didn't press the issue too hard. When I thought about it the idea gave me a lot of excitement. I suppose it was echoes from way back of seeing Barry masturbate in the cinema, or noticing that Terry was ogling my cleavage at the bowls. Jason took another set of pictures one night, I was really daring in those and played with a vibrator, and when we had finished, I told him – as long as he was discreet – he could show a couple of those pictures to his colleagues.'

She chuckles and admits, 'We had a bloody fantastic night's sex after that. I didn't think about it at the time but afterwards I realised I was very aroused by the idea of somebody else seeing pictures of me playing with a vibrator. When Jason got back from work the next day I practically fell on him trying to find out what had happened and who he'd shown them to.

'He was laughing at my enthusiasm. But, when he told me about showing them to two of his subordinates, I could tell he was just as excited as me. We ended up putting the kids to bed early that night and having another bloody fantastic night as he told me again about how one of them had been grinning at the picture and licking his lips and the other had been covering his groin because he had a bloody big hard-on. I said I wanted to take more pictures and Jason was very happy to do that.' Talking about those early photo sessions fires Joyce with a passionate enthusiasm. Her hand-gestures become more animated and her cheeks fill with a colour that isn't quite a blush, but is certainly close.

'We did a set of photos with me wearing a thong and bra, far more revealing than I would ordinarily wear. And I was getting very wet every time Jason's camera flashed because I knew that I was posing for his friends. I got him to do me again after the photo session and then spent another long day waiting to find out what his friends had thought of the pictures.

'We went on like that for a couple of months. Jason didn't take pictures every night. When you have a couple of kids in the house you don't have much time for yourselves. But I'd go out and buy myself some new underwear one day, and Jason would photograph me wearing it the next night. And then he'd take the pictures in the following day and we'd be having more great sex as he told me how aroused his colleagues had been.

'I was getting excited by the idea of other men finding my body attractive. Attractive enough to give them a hard-on. When you have a couple of kids, and you know your tummy has a bit of a paunch, you start to think that you're no longer attractive or desirable. It doesn't help that every magazine shows a woman who looks absolutely gorgeous. Jason's pictures seemed very flattering to me but it was true I'd put a lot of effort into getting my figure back and keeping myself looking trim. Knowing that pictures of me were exciting his friends was like an affirmation that all that hard work had been worthwhile.' Joyce pauses to consider this and then nods as though pleased with the way she has summarised her thoughts. 'Jason would come back from the office after showing off my pictures and he'd tell me who had a hard-on, and what sort of comments I'd received, and then we'd go mad for another session of sex if the kids were off and maybe take another set of more revealing pictures.

'I'm not sure how much further it could have gone. But it was brought to a head when Jason invited Tony, one of his colleagues, round for a meal one weekend. Tony was the one who, according to Jason, always got the biggest hard-ons looking at my pictures. When I asked Jason what Tony might be expecting as well as a meal, he promised me that Tony wasn't expecting anything.' She smiles sourly and adds, 'But I could see he was thinking, "Let's see how the evening goes."

'I'm not ashamed to admit that I was aroused when we prepared for that evening. Tony had seen pictures of me that were incredibly revealing. He'd seen pictures of me in a bikini. He'd seen pictures of me in a thong and matching bra. He'd seen pictures of me naked and he'd seen the ones where I'd been playing with a dildo. The fact that he'd supposedly got a hard-on every time made me sure he found me desirable. But I still had no idea how the evening was going to go. Tony was a polite dinner guest. I could see he was admiring me from the start of the evening but that was OK. The conversation was mainly about the office where Tony and Jason worked to start with, and then it moved on to family holidays and the like. Jason was clearing the plates into the kitchen, and taking his time about it, when I first realised he'd left me alone with Tony.

'Tony said he'd enjoyed my pictures. I tried to dismiss the comment with a laugh but, as soon as he said that, there was a lot of sexual tension in the air. My nipples went hard and I could feel myself getting very wet. I told Tony that Jason and I took a lot of pictures and I was glad he'd enjoyed them. He was sat close to me and he whispered that he'd tugged off a couple of times, thinking about my pictures. He even said that Jason had let him copy one of the pictures and he used it all the time when he was tugging off at home.

'To my relief, Jason came back in then. He saw Tony was whispering in my ear and I said, "Tony's just been telling me that he enjoys my pictures. You'll have to invite him to one of the photo sessions we have. I'm sure he'd enjoy seeing what goes on." Jason gave me a look of such gratitude. Tony could only gape.

'Jason said, "We could always have a photo session this evening, if you wanted." It wasn't what I'd expected to happen that evening. I don't know what I'd been expecting but I hadn't thought I would be stripping off in front of the camera while Jason and Tony watched.' Joyce blushes deeply as she says this and reveals an embarrassed smile. 'Well, I suppose I had thought that it might happen. But I hadn't really believed it would happen. It was very arousing. I could have had an orgasm in the moment that Jason first made the suggestion. When the three of us went to Jason's makeshift photography studio in the spare room, I was practically trembling with excitement. Nevertheless, when we got into the spare room, I made sure they were both aware of my conditions.

' "I'm only going to strip," I explained. "I'm sorry, Tony, but I'm not going to let you do it to me. I won't do anything like that. But, other than that, I want you to enjoy the photo session as much as you like."

'Tony asked me what I meant by that and I explained that I was very aroused and I was probably going to touch myself while Jason was taking the pictures. The studio has a single bed where I've posed for a few of the photos and I've been comfortable enough in there before to lie down and touch myself. I told Tony he could tug himself while he watched and I wouldn't be offended. And that was what started a truly bloody fantastic night.

'I took my time over the strip. I'd made sure I was wearing some pretty underwear when I got dressed for the evening. And I made sure Jason got some great pictures of me peeling off my clothes. Both of the boys were very excited. Tony kept murmuring things like, "Bloody marvellous!" and, "Isn't she fantastic?" I basked in the praise and just got wetter.

'Jason's first digital camera would only take a dozen or so pictures on hi-res before he had to upload them to the PC. He went out of the room and left Tony alone with me while he did that the first time. I'd undressed down to my underwear and I was feeling wonderfully vulnerable being alone in the studio with him.

'I asked Tony if he was enjoying the photo shoot and he said it was good. I asked him if he'd show me how good he thought the show was. He pulled out this huge hard-on that really put Jason to shame. As soon as I saw it I began to wonder if I hadn't been a bit silly saying I wasn't going to have sex with him. But I stuck to my word because you hear so many things about diseases and illnesses and other unpleasantness and I didn't want to spoil something as good as what I was enjoying with the unnecessary risk of catching something.

'I did put my hand around Tony's cock. Jason came back into the room while I was rubbing my palm over the helmet. He had this big grin on his face and said, "Bloody hell! The boy's deformed!" Laughing, Joyce gestures with her hands to show Tony's impressive length and insists, 'He really was a big boy.' It's difficult not to be impressed by the distance between her open palms.

'The three of us were laughing as we carried on with the second part of the photo shoot. Tony kept his hard-on out while I removed my underwear. Jason kept telling me to move this way and move that way, shove my bum towards the camera and then lose the bra. It took another dozen photographs before I was naked and Jason needed to go and upload them again.

'And I was left alone with Tony again while he did that.

'It was hard to make idle chitchat under those circumstances. Tony said he was desperate to do it to me. I said I was desperate for someone to do it to me, but I couldn't let him. He said he understood, and respected my limitations. But you could also see it was hard on the poor boy.

'I called him over to the bed where I was lying and said he could come on my tits if he wanted. His cock twitched when I made the suggestion and watching that made my arousal skyrocket. I didn't know how much longer Jason was going to be, but I told Tony, if it would make things easier for him while he was tugging himself, I would provide a little lubrication. Then, because his cock was close to my face, I put my mouth around it and sucked on the end.

'I still had my lips around his cock when Jason came back into the room. The final part of the photo shoot went in a blur. I started touching myself. I had my first orgasm very quickly, and Jason got some wonderful pictures of my face twisted with pleasure. Tony was stood nearby, tugging his big length vigorously, and then Jason came and stood by the opposite side of the bed and got out his own hard-on.

'I was laid beneath them because they were both standing, and I was watching two handsome men tugging off as they admired me. It didn't take much for me to have my second orgasm. I think I'd climaxed before the first spurt of come had splashed on my boobs.' Joyce shivers a little as she says this and it's apparent, even though the first photo shoot occurred more than a decade earlier, the memory is still potent and pleasurable.

'Jason gave Tony a couple of the pictures he'd taken – as a memento really – and we promised him we'd have another meal again soon. And we have done. Tony calls around every month or so. Even now that he's married. And Tony was only the first of Jason's colleagues that got to attend one of our photo shoots. There have probably been a couple of dozen of them over the years and maybe a dozen or so of them still call round every now and then.

'It's not swinging. I don't have sex with any of them. The most I've ever done is provide a little extra lubrication for the man who's watching me. And I don't think I'll ever do more than that. I don't think I'll ever need to. Jason says it's the fulfilment of his fantasies to see other men admiring me and I do enjoy the attention. Even though I'm now an old married woman, it satisfies me to see how much I can still arouse other men.'

Kara is a forty-eight-year-old office administrator and lives in Cumbria with her present partner, Kevin. Kara was a swinger for five years at the end of her late thirties but this involvement with the lifestyle was cut short by the end of her marriage.

Kara: 'I'd been into swinging before I met Kevin. When I told him about my past his first reaction was not what I expected.'

Our interview takes place in a swingers' club. It's a midweek afternoon, Kara is a friend of the owner as well as a regular customer, and she thought it would be the ideal place for us to talk about her view of swinging. Without anyone else in the club, except for a couple of cleaners who study us warily as they work their way around the room, the swingers' club looks surprisingly mundane. But, because we're alone and Kara is in a familiar environment, she seems comfortable with the subject matter.

'I'd been swinging for five years with Alan. He met someone else and so we agreed to part and, after that, I simply fell away from the scene. He was still swinging, as was his new wife, and I knew there was a chance I could meet them at a party and have sex with them both if we were all of a mind.' She shakes her head and says, 'But I could also see that wouldn't be sensible for my own sanity. You don't go through a divorce just to have sex with your partner at a naughty schoolgirls night. Without Alan I figured swinging wouldn't be the same. And I didn't want to go to parties and be constantly on the lookout for him in an attempt to avoid him. So I dropped out of the swinging scene and, six months later, I enrolled on a couple of college courses. I did that so I had something else to do with my spare time rather than brood about the lack of parties. And, while I was probably playing with my Rabbit [vibrator] more than was healthy, I tried to become respectable and proper.' Kara makes this last remark with dry humour. She is dressed casually for our interview, wearing jeans and a loose sweatshirt. But there is a devilish glint in her eye that suggests her personal preferences never stray to the respectable and proper.

'It wasn't easy. One of the other students at college asked me out on a date during the second week of term. Out of habit, I almost ended up shagging him on the first night. I kept myself "pure" for about three or four dates, and then we finally got down to it and he was pretty good. We sort of fell into boyfriend/girlfriend mode and that was when I discovered the problem about honesty. While I'd been with Alan we'd always told each other what we were doing with other people and who we'd been with and everything.' She falls silent and reflects on this for a moment before saying, 'Well, I suppose he kept some secrets before he told me he wanted a separation, but other than that, we were pretty honest with each other. When we were alone we'd talk about all the things we'd done and remind each other about high points and exciting times. I'd talk about him and one of our friends from the local club when they DP'd [double-penetration] me – that was always one of my favourites – and he'd talk about me eating out the club's hostess. Those honest conversations were the sort of foreplay that you only get when you're actively involved in the swinging community and I'd pretty much taken that level of honesty for granted.

'So, when this guy from college started to ask me about my sex life prior to him, I saw there was going to be a problem I hadn't thought about before. The whole idea of a sexual history was alien to me because my sexual history had always been an open book to Alan. He knew about the gangbangs, the threeways and the girl-on-girl stuff.' Kara chuckles and says, 'I'd never had a sexual history as it were:

it had always been more like current affairs. But it was different with the college guy. His sexual history included about a dozen women. And so did mine.'

The interview is paused while we retrieve bottles of mineral water from the club's dry bar. Kara drinks hers straight from the bottle before continuing to talk about her college romance. 'I'm probably doing him a great injustice here,' she admits. 'He was a nice enough guy, the sex was good, even if it wasn't very imaginative, and he did try hard. But I was so used to swinging – and the rules of swinging – I had difficulty relating to him honestly. One of the main unwritten rules about swinging is that you don't talk to "*the normals*" about what you do at a party. It's not like there's a big secrecy regarding swinging and swingers' parties. It's just, if you start to tell your friends and colleagues what you've been doing, they start to look at you as though you're filth, and then gossip about the fact that you're a cock-monster.

'I wanted to tell him about the swinging and everything. But every time I tried I could just see it was likely to bring the relationship to an abrupt and unpleasant end. I know that probably sounds like thinly disguised cowardice but I couldn't tell him all the things I'd done because he wouldn't have understood that it was just sex and most of it meant nothing.' Kara takes a long drag at her bottle of mineral water. Opening a window she lights a cigarette before resuming the conversation. 'He'd been with a dozen women in his life and loved every one of them,' she quips. 'I'd been with a dozen blokes in one weekend and loved every second of it. We had such differing attitudes towards sex that I could see it was going to be a big issue if he ever found out about my swinging. So I broke up with him and started seeing another guy, and kept everything non-sexual for about six months.

'It was hard work. Frustrating. And expensive on batteries for my Rabbit. But I thought it would be the best way of dealing with the whole *sexual history* thing. Then, when we finally did end up in the bedroom, I discovered the sex wasn't too great. Again, I think that was down to me. When we first started doing it I could imagine us having the conversation about sexual history and I thought, "He's going to wonder why I was giving this away at parties and made him wait half a year." So I broke off from him before we faced the embarrassment of *not* having that conversation.' She finishes her cigarette before continuing, crushing it firmly into a glass ashtray.

'A few months after him I met Kevin. Rather than worry about stuff that was outside my control I just let things develop between us. We ended up in bed together eventually. Sooner than is probably proper, but not so soon it looked like I had just spontaneously jumped his bones.

'And he was pretty damned good. He's imaginative, considerate and passionate. Everything you could want from a man in bed. But when the subject came to what sort of things we'd done before we met I said I didn't want to talk about it. I think he'd only asked me what my best sexual experience was, but I couldn't tell him that because it would lead to other questions and I figured the answers would be more than he could handle. My best sexual experience was being DP'd by Alan and one of the doormen from the club where we used to go. Alan had a good-sized cock and the doorman was slightly thicker. Having one in my pussy and the other in my anus made me feel stretched to the point of tearing but it also made me come harder than I've ever come before or since. But I couldn't tell Kevin about that because he'd wonder what other things I'd done, if I'd ever seen this doorman since, and why my ex-husband was familiar with the bouncer from a swingers' club.'

Brushing the hair from her forehead, Kara says, 'Kevin was cool about my not wanting to discuss the subject, but it started to limit the sorts of things we could talk about and that did prove to be a problem. I'd always enjoyed the verbal foreplay of talking about past events and stuff. It never failed to get me wet. It was something I did with Alan not just as foreplay, but while we were in the middle of a good fucking session. But, with Kevin, every time one of us tried a new position or suggested doing something we hadn't previously tried together – bondage, watersports, anal – a whole load of previous experiences were lurking at the back of my thoughts, and colouring whatever I wanted to say.

'Eventually I said we had to talk. He seemed like a decent guy, and we were enjoying each other's company big time. He was the most satisfying sexual partner I'd had since splitting with Alan and I genuinely liked his company, whether we were having sex or not. We sat down for what I thought would be a heavy discussion. I said, "I want to be honest with you. I've not told you about my sexual history because I didn't want to scare you away. The truth is, before I met you, I was into swinging. With my former partner I must have had sex with hundreds of men and dozens of women. I'm telling you all this because we've been talking about what sort of things we enjoy doing in bed and you wanted to know what my best ever experience was. I wanted to tell you that my best ever experience was a threeway with Alan and one of the doormen from a local swingers' club. The pair of them spit-roasted me, DP'd me and basically spent hours making me come my brains out almost constantly. I'm telling you this because I like you and I respect you and I want to be totally honest with you."'

Kara laughs when it's suggested that the discussion was very one-sided.

'It was sure to be one-sided,' she admits. 'Before I said a word I knew he could either say, "Fuck! Yes!" or "Fuck off!" But he didn't say anything at first. After I'd finished talking it was like a great relief coming off my shoulders. At first I thought, whether he's happy with that or not, at least I'm not carrying around this burden of guilt any more. But, the longer he sat there, not saying anything, the more I started to panic. I didn't know if he was going to be pissed at me, angry, accepting or disgusted. Eventually I said, "If you're not happy with that we can talk about it. But I figure we know each other well enough now to be honest. I don't want you to think I'm keeping secrets."

'He asked why I'd given up swinging and I told him about Alan and the whole complicated thing with the parties and Alan's new partner and everything, then he asked if I'd missed the swinging during the time since I'd split with Alan.' Kara releases a long, soft whistle, then lights another cigarette. 'I thought hard about that before answering. I'd rehearsed answers to a lot of questions in my head before we had the conversation but "Had I missed the swinging?" wasn't one of the ones I'd thought Kevin might ask. When I realised he was still waiting for an answer, I figured I ought to be honest and I told him I did miss the swinging. I told him I'd missed it a lot sometimes. There's not much as satisfying as going to a party and going down on a good-looking woman, while a group of admiring men tug themselves off and cheer you on. Sexually, I don't think there's anything better than being sandwiched between two guys who are filling both your holes. When it comes to favourite sexual positions I think a threeway with lots of DP has to rank as my number one. So I said that I had missed it, but I didn't have the guts to go it alone.' She blows a long stream of cigarette smoke towards the open window before saying, 'That was when Kevin asked me if I'd introduce him to swinging. He said, since I was being honest with him, and admitting all about my past, he thought he should be honest with me and admit that he'd always wanted to try swinging, but he'd never had the guts to go alone either. He'd never been able to ask a partner if she would be interested in trying it. And he said the idea of seeing me come while I was having a DP really turned him on.

'I can't tell you what a relief it was to hear those words.

'We started gently at first, just with a threeway and then with a same-room swap. Kevin was quite satisfied with those events.' Kara pauses and laughs, then admits, 'Well, that's an understatement. He hasn't stopped talking about them since. But he has the right perspective on the swinging in that it's just fun – nothing serious – only sex. I've taken him to a few parties since and we're becoming known as a fun couple. And, while it's good to be back swinging and getting proper sexual satisfaction, it's great to have a man in my life who accepts all the things that I like and helps me to get them.'

Lorraine is forty-seven and Liam is forty-five. The couple have been married for twenty-one years and swinging for two. The couple's interest in swinging developed shortly after their second child moved out of the family home and left them alone, as a couple, for the first time in twenty-two years.

Lorraine: 'Whenever we talked about our sexual fantasies, Liam would always say the same thing: he wanted to see me with another woman. I don't know why he wanted to see that. I've spoken to several women, read loads of books and stuff, and I know it's a common male fantasy, probably the commonest. But, even though I was OK with indulging Liam's fantasy and I'd always liked the idea of going with a woman, I had no idea where to begin.'

Our conversation takes place at Lorraine and Liam's home and, because there's a match on, Liam has left us alone in the kitchen so he can watch the TV in a different room. Lorraine is a slender woman, delicate and comparatively petite. She exudes a surprising air of confidence and capability but modestly attributes this to having spent two decades being a mother. Her observations on the difficulty in meeting single bisexual females correspond with similar remarks from lots of frustrated female swingers.

'Liam was no help on that front. He didn't have lots of female friends all wanting to lick me from here to next Tuesday. But I can't complain about that because I was at an equal loss for how to start. I'd never thought of any of my friends as potential sexual conquests. And there was no way I was going to risk the scandal of approaching any of them about the subject, or making a coy suggestion and hoping something developed from there.

'So, for a long time, it stayed as just a fantasy.

'We kept talking about various ways we might make something happen. Liam bought a couple of magazines, *Desire* and *Forum* I think. I bought copies of *Loot* and we went through their classifieds on a regular basis. But there was never anything in them that appealed to both of us. We looked at a few places online but, back then, we had child protection software on our computer and that meant we couldn't see anything interesting on the internet.'

When it's suggested that the child protection software could have been disabled or deactivated, Lorraine shakes her head and explains that neither she nor Liam are computer-minded. A friend had installed the child protection software and asking him to teach them how to switch it off would have been embarrassing. Now their children have grown up and left home they have a new computer without child protection software. But, back then, it was a different situation. 'The way it was set up wouldn't allow us to see anything that might help,' Lorraine continues. 'But Liam kept on saying it was something he wanted to see. We experimented with other fantasies in the interim. We tried tying each other up, which was OK. He spanked my bum a few times and I spanked him a few times. And that was all quite exciting.'

Ironically, Lorraine says this without any inflection of emotion. She smirks when this is mentioned and points out that the bondage and spanking were exciting at the time, but she's not going to have an orgasm just talking about those events. Going back to the subject of Liam's fantasies, she says, 'While he wanted to see me with a woman, I admitted I had always fancied seeing him with a man. I don't think he warmed to that idea very much. He didn't spend half as much time trying to make that one happen. But he did say, if it was going to get me aroused, he would certainly try it. And then we got back on with trying to find a way of getting me into bed with a woman.

'The epiphany happened when we were reading an article about a swingers' club. A local place was causing a big controversy because they'd applied for an alcohol licence. A big argument had started with one of the local churches saying the swingers' club should be closed down. We both felt like idiots for not having thought about a swingers' club before and, as soon as we'd decided that was what we wanted, we arranged to go to one that wasn't caught up in a controversy with the local church.'

Settling herself comfortably in her seat, Lorraine says, 'The only thing that happened that first night was that I got a kiss. Lots of other things could have happened. It was a lively place and there were some very attractive couples in the club. But I was really nervous and that was working against me. Not all of the women there were what you'd call lookers but most of them were attractive. The way that they carried themselves, as though they knew they were sexy, certainly made them seem very exciting and I think that was what started to intimidate me. There were some couples kissing. There were others doing more than that. One woman was sucking a guy's cock in the corner of the room. Some of the couples fell into conversations and then disappeared out of the main club area, going upstairs to the bedrooms. It was very busy but I think, because everyone else there seemed to know what they were doing, I felt like a fish out of water.' Glancing pointedly in the direction of the room where her husband is watching TV, she says, 'Liam kept nodding at women, asking, "Do you fancy her?" And I'd be saying, "She's OK. If you like." But I wouldn't take it any further than that and I started to draw into myself.

'Then Natalie and her husband joined us at our table. We'd never met them before. They just stood by our table, said, "Mind if we join you?" and before we could respond they were pulling up chairs and sitting down.' Lorraine's grin is suddenly broad and, although there had been no emotion in her voice when she talked about bondage and BDSM with her husband, she now talks with a tone of approval. 'Natalie was gorgeous. She was probably the photo-fit of everything I would have wanted in a woman if I'd been asked to describe what I was looking for. She was my height. She was wearing stockings and a low-cut top to show off her enormous boobs. She had a really dirty laugh and said lots of things that, when I thought about them afterwards, they had my gusset soaked.

'But nothing happened that night. Natalie asked what we were looking for. Eventually, after a lot of stammering, I said I wanted to do something with a woman while my husband watched. Natalie said that was the same reason why she and her husband had come to the club. I couldn't meet her eye while she was talking and I thought she would think I was either rude, retarded or just not interested. She asked if it was our first time and when I said yes she wrote down a number on the back of a card and said I should give her a call when I'd got over my first-night nerves. Then she leaned over and I thought, *She's going to give me a kiss on the cheek and say goodnight*.

'Instead, Natalie gave me this big, long, lingering kiss. She didn't go over the top, sticking her tongue down my throat or any of those porn movie things. She just gave me this really passionate, sensual kiss. Our lips were constantly together and as it went on, I started thinking, *I'm kissing a woman*.

'Liam was watching and he told me after that he'd almost come in his pants when she kissed me. I'd known that much because I could see his eyes were practically standing out on their stalks. Natalie stood up and tapped the card I still held, saying, "Call me when you're ready." And, right then, I could have come in my own pants.' Lorraine lowers her gaze as she makes this statement of honest rudeness and it's flattering to know that she's being so candid about what happened at that first party. 'We went home shortly after that and had some pretty good sex,' she continues. 'It was exciting to think that we'd been to a swingers' club, even though nothing had really happened. But I was very very wet just thinking about the way Natalie had kissed me. I suppose I was being silly but I thought there had been a lot of chemistry between us.' She shrugs and adds, 'I can't explain it any better than that.

'Nevertheless, I came close to throwing her number away without calling. We'd tried the swingers' clubs, they weren't quite the right atmosphere for me to feel comfortable, and Liam agreed that we weren't going to do things that we didn't feel comfortable doing. He still wanted to see me going all the way with a woman, and after Natalie's kiss it was something I wanted more badly than ever. But I figured nothing was going to happen at a swingers' club so there was no reason for my holding on to her number.

'I gave her a call to tell her that much. She was just as exciting on the phone as she had been in the club. I was wet as soon as I heard her voice and I thought, if I'm going to do it with any woman, I want it to be this woman. I reminded her who I was, she remembered me, and asked if I'd overcome my first-night nerves. I said I hadn't overcome them, I didn't think the swingers' clubs were right for me, but I just wanted to thank her for the kiss because it had been exciting. She said that if we met again we could do more than just kiss. I was going weak on the other end of the phone. I told her I really wanted to, but I'd probably be just as nervous at the swingers' club as I had been when we last saw each other. She suggested the four of us meet at a regular pub and just chat about what it was that I was looking for.

'Without consulting Liam, I agreed. We arranged to meet at a pub that wasn't too far away and I told Liam about it as soon as he got home from work. He was over the moon. I told him that most likely we would just be talking and nothing would happen. But it was obvious he thought we were going to go all the way and nothing was going to stop us this time.

'When we met them at the pub I thought my pessimistic assessment of the evening was going to prove right. Natalie and her husband were both wearing jeans and T-shirts – nothing particularly sexy or glamorous. She still looked stunning but she also looked ultra-casual. We had a drink together, chatted about various things from the weather to the news, and then Natalie asked what it was we had wanted to do.

'I told her again that I wanted to do something with a woman. And I said I wanted to do it while Liam was watching. I explained that the atmosphere at the club had been too much for me and she asked, "Do you think the atmosphere will be better if you come back to ours?"

'It was a twenty minute drive back to their place and I half expected my mood to calm down by the time we reached there. I thought common sense or my earlier fears might come back into play by the time we got to their house. But Natalie put us at our ease as soon as we arrived. We settled down in the lounge, Natalie directed Liam to the settee next to her husband and she kept me standing with her in the middle of the room. Instead of looking at me she addressed the guys and said, "This is going to get really hot and horny, so you might as well get your dicks out now."'

Lorraine glances towards the door through which her husband had disappeared and winks conspiratorially. 'Neither of them hesitated and I watched Liam and Natalie's husband pull their cocks out and start stroking them. It was a really exciting moment – I hadn't expected anything like that and it took all the pressure off me. I got a good long look at Natalie's husband's cock, and I was wondering if I'd get a chance to touch it before the night was over. That was when Natalie touched me on the shoulder and said, "Do you want to kiss me now?"

'So we kissed.

'Well, we did a lot more than kiss. She got me really worked up again and we slowly undressed each other while our husbands watched and wanked. I got to touch her boobs, and then I got to suck on them and play with them. I got to take her panties off, then eat her pussy. In short, I got to do everything I'd always thought would happen if I got naked with another woman. It was our proper introduction to swinging – the first time we got naked with another couple, but it wasn't our last. Although we never saw Natalie and her husband again after that, going to their house, and getting close to them on such comfortable territory, gave me the confidence to suggest we revisit the swingers' club.' Lorraine smiles contentedly and confides that she is truly happy with this development in her sex life. 'Since that first time we try to do something with another couple once a month, whether it's going to a club, or meeting a couple from the classifieds or online. We've done much more since that first experience: swapped with couples, had a full-on threesome, and even attended a small orgy. But we wouldn't have done any of it if Natalie and her husband hadn't been kind enough to take the time to patiently introduce us to swinging.'

SWAPPING

> **First Time Couple** (mid-40s) seek similar
> or younger for same-room swap.
> Cleanliness and *discretion* expected and
> assured. P.O. Box AL005

One of the most misunderstood aspects of the swinging community is the diversity of each individual's interpretation of what comprises swinging. Swinging is something of an enigma to those outside this close-knit community. There is a paucity of reliable information relating to the contemporary swinging scene in the UK. As observed in the introduction to this book, the majority of studies have been carried out in the US and, until recently, these were conducted on surprisingly small test groups.

Non-swingers often labour under the misconception that every swinger is willing to participate in any sexual act – regardless of its complexities, morality or depravity. Non-swingers believe that the swinging community consists of decadent individuals who have no limits on what they will do for satisfaction. Members of the swinging community are perceived as both specific and general deviants and some interesting studies have shown that non-swingers wrongly associate swingers with excessive drug-taking, antisocial behaviour and many other undesirable qualities. But, aside from deviating from the sexual norm, it has been shown that generally and specifically, swingers are no more deviant than non-swingers. They vary from expected norms only in their attitudes to sex and sexuality.

Many of the couples I spoke with did insist, 'Orgies are the best.' The enthusiasm for 'a mass of naked arms and legs all writhing together' was frequently stated as the epitome of a successful party/night out. But, even in these circumstances, there are still varying degrees of participation. For instance, I spoke with two couples who insisted that orgies were the ultimate form of swinging. Both couples were from a similar age bracket, had been married and swinging for similar lengths of time, and conducted their swinging through a mixture of clubs and private contact ads. When speaking to the first couple, the husband explained, 'The last orgy was particularly good because I got my cock sucked by this gorgeous guy.' But the husband of the second couple said, 'The last orgy was spoilt for me because a guy started sucking my cock.'

The diversity does not just extend to heterosexual vs homosexual encounters. Some swingers will only visit clubs; others will only use contact ads. And, just to make the diversity complete, others will combine the two as and when the mood suits them. A complex mixture of sexual preferences and physical attraction govern the intimacy that will occur when two couples meet. And the entire meeting will be controlled by the influence of previous sexual experiences; the knowledge of shared sexual fantasies and desires; and the ability to successfully relate the necessary aspects of this information to another couple.

The diverse ways that swingers interact is best exemplified by the different attitudes to something as simple as same-room or separate-room play. Couples looking to meet with other couples will often explicitly state whether they wish to swing in the same room as their partner or conduct their activities in a separate room. The reasons for this distinction are numerous but the arguments for separate-room swinging usually include shyness, propriety and simple convenience. The motives for same-room swinging are equally varied and include many of the same reasons. The ostensibly minor difference of same-room/separate-room play is mentioned prominently in this chapter because it shows, while non-swingers believe each member of the swinging community will do anything in their pursuit of sexual satisfaction, many members of the swinging community are bound by this simple and self-imposed restriction.

Maria and Marlon are fifty-eight and sixty-one respectively and have been swinging for approximately ten years. Maria describes herself as a full-time housewife and retired mother. Marlon works as a consultant engineer for a construction company. The couple have been married for more than thirty years and live in Leicestershire.

Maria: 'We don't look for the ultimate but, if it happens, it happens. Our advert says, "Mid-fifties couple seeks similar for same-room fun," and that's basically what we're looking for.' She produces a recent copy of *Desire* and points to the advert in the couples' section. Question marks, circled adverts and big red crosses on the page suggest that Maria and Marlon have been through this issue meticulously. 'I know it's not strictly true to describe us as a mid-fifties couple,' Maria admits sheepishly. 'Fifty-eight is past the middle of mid-fifties and sixty-one is definitely past that range. But we're both young at heart and I do believe that age is just numbers. We got into swinging about ten years ago and it's proved to be the best thing we ever did as a couple.

'Usually we arrange to meet a couple for a drink, get to know them, and then invite them round to our home. By the time you've had a few drinks together, you can get an idea as to whether or not anything is going to happen, or whether you'll want it to happen. Then, once we're back home, we settle down to watch some porn, or have a sexy chat, and we see where everything leads.' Maria describes all this in such a matter-of-fact way it makes the experience sound more comfortable and social than erotic.

'It was Marlon's idea to try swinging,' she confides. 'Our sex life had always been all right but nothing to write home about. We'd just moved to this bungalow after our eldest got her own place. When we were decorating the new bedroom Marlon said it might be fun to add a little spice to our sex life now that we had the privacy of no kids cluttering the house. When we talked about it, it turned out we both fancied the idea of bringing other people into our sex life or at least getting into other people's sex lives. Neither of us had anyone specific in mind, you understand. We just wanted to get involved with other people in general.

'We placed our first advert in a magazine. We were mid-forties back then with me at forty-eight and Marlon at fifty-one.' She smiles self-consciously at this recurring anomaly and again insists that age is just numbers. 'We got a few calls and I thought they were all very exciting. We were on the phone to strangers, they were asking us what sort of things we were looking for and we explained exactly what we were after. I think we met two or three couples from the first advert and we started feeling our way into a routine from there.

'Usually it would start with a meet at the pub. It still does. We have a drink and a chat about bland stuff like the weather and their journey and that sort of thing. Then, once we're all comfortable with each other, we start talking about sex. We follow the same routine nowadays and I still find it enormously exciting. As soon as the conversation moves on to sex I get a thrill from the whole situation. I get aroused. Everybody is lowering their voices. I'm usually blushing. Marlon is touching my leg under the table. And even if the couple don't want to come back to ours, I know I'll be having fun with Marlon when we get home.'

Marlon is in the room with us and he chuckles. Maria blushes and passes him the sort of silencing glare that would start a fight between strangers, but is a sign of loving resignation in established married couples. Maria passes him the copy of *Desire*, tells him to make himself useful and go through it again, and then patiently resumes our interview.

'The conversations in the pub start off vague. One of us will ask, "So what sort of things do you like doing?" And the answer is nearly always something risqué. If the couple have asked the question, Marlon always says, "I like to watch my wife go down on another man." That's enough to make me very wet. And if the other couple say anything similar, we know we're going to have a very good night.

'Sometimes we'll have another drink before we suggest moving on. Other times, if we all seem very eager, Marlon will suggest that we finish the conversation back at ours. The pub's only a short car-ride away. It's walking distance really but no one in their right mind would leave their car in a pub car park. And then the four of us will get together in our lounge and Marlon will put on a porn video in the background while the four of us chat and we all get properly acquainted.'

From his corner of the room Marlon translates that this means they fuck. Maria shushes him and insists that's not what she meant at all. Sometimes sex happens, she explains, and sometimes it doesn't. When she said they all get properly acquainted she meant that they get to know each other better. Dismissing her husband's contribution, telling him to read his comic, she clears her throat to continue.

'I always wear a skirt and no knickers when we go out to meet another couple. It's something I've always done, no matter what the weather, and I find it makes my mood friskier than ever. Wearing a skirt and no knickers makes me very conscious that I'm exposed down there and it's a constant reminder of what we're planning to do. It also means, when we get back home, it's really easy to "accidentally" flash myself at our guests. That, and the porn video in the background, usually help us get things back into the frisky mood we were all sharing before we left the pub.

'With one couple, she saw I'd got no knickers on, she stood up and said, "Maria's not wearing knickers, so I'm going to take mine off too." Then she wriggled out of her knickers, kicked them across the room and lifted her skirt to show us that she'd taken them off. That started a really good night. We've seen that couple several times since and she makes a point of asking about my knickers when we meet up in the pub. There've been a couple of times where she's flashed under her skirt at me in the pub, to show that she's not wearing any. She sometimes flashes herself at Marlon, as her way of saying that she's bored of the pub and wants to get back to ours so we can do something more.'

From his corner of the room, Marlon explains that he's never complained about their friend flashing him in the room. Maria ignores him.

'Then the evening will move out of the pub and carry on from there,' she continues. 'At ours, it all depends what the other couple are wanting really. We're fairly easy-going and, as long as we can all four stay in the same room, we're happy to do most things. There's a couple of things we don't want to do but we've usually told them what we don't do either on the phone or in the pub. If things seem to be going slowly, Marlon will say again that he enjoys watching me go down on other men. There haven't been many fellas that have refused that invitation.' Maria glances at her husband and whispers, 'And I do enjoy having a man's penis in my mouth. I like that for a number of reasons. I know Marlon gets a lot out of it. He's almost come in his pants when I've had a stranger's penis in my mouth and I've winked at him. Knowing my husband is so aroused is one of the main thrills. But it's also exciting because it's so sexual and so different from what we had when we were having polite evenings with non-swinging friends while the kids lived at home. It's like I've been given a chance to start having sex again, but now I'm old enough to enjoy it and appreciate it, it seems better than when I was young.' She glances again at Marlon and insists, 'Having a stranger's penis in your mouth is very arousing.

'I always use condoms for penetrative sex. But I don't use them for oral sex. Never. I don't like the taste of condoms. But I do like the taste of a warm, sticky penis.' The interview breaks off for a moment as we discuss the health risks that are implicated by this activity. Maria is not the first swinger who has expressed distaste for using condoms in oral sex and we argue, politely, about the potential dangers. Maria concedes that it would be safer to use condoms for everything but she insists that the taste is so unpleasant it spoils her arousal. 'I suppose I'm putting myself at some sort of health risk,' she admits. 'But I always figure, I'm likely to have my tongue in his wife's vagina by the end of the evening, and there's no doubt in my mind that they will have had unprotected sex on their way to meeting us, so I'm not subjecting myself to any greater risk than I was planning. But I don't think it's that great a risk.

'We must have seen more than a hundred couples since we first started swinging and the worst I've suffered in all that time is a sore throat and a dose of flu. The sore throat might not have been caused by me sucking another man's cock. You can pick up those bugs anywhere and it's as likely that I got that from a dirty glass at the pub than from having a stranger's penis in my mouth. Besides, I try not to think about diseases and things on the night because that really would spoil the mood.'

She brushes away this side-topic with a flutter of her hands. Marlon sighs heavily from the corner of the room and it's apparent that he is also pleased that the conversation is moving back on track. 'The chances are, if I'm sucking our guest's penis, his wife will be doing something similar to Marlon. That's another exciting thing that always makes me wet. When you read about swingers in the papers it usually makes out that husbands and wives don't care about each other and that there's no love between them. But that's not true at all. When you're sucking a man's penis and making your husband proud and excited, and your husband is getting sucked by another woman, but he's staring fondly across the room at you, it affirms the strength of the love between you. It shows that you can trust each other and you can share things that other couples would find impossible to share. I don't suppose everyone sees it like that. But that's the way we see it.

'And it's not the main thing that goes through my mind when we're getting sexually involved with another couple. Usually I'm caught up in the moment and moaning and swallowing the taste of another man's penis. But it's one of the things that I always think about afterwards when Marlon's making love to me after they've gone and we're on our own.'

From behind his copy of *Desire*, Marlon says that it's not always oral sex and Maria points out that she hadn't said it was *always* oral sex. Just that is was *often* oral sex. Shaking her head at her husband's unsolicited input she takes a deep breath and says, 'It doesn't always work out with oral sex at the start of the night. Every time we meet another couple it's different really. Some couples just want to watch us, or we'll watch them. Sometimes there'll be no physical contact between us. We'll just sit in front of the porn video in various states of undress, me touching Marlon, Marlon touching me, and them touching each other. Sometimes it will be us girls playing together while the fellas watch. That's always a laugh. I don't think I'm bisexual. I don't mind licking a vagina, or playing with boobs. And I've had more than one woman make me have an orgasm by doing the same thing for me. But I don't expressly look forward to having that happen when we've organised an evening. We don't say I'm bisexual in the advert. We just play the evening as it goes and that seems to happen fairly often. Of course, I'm open to most suggestions, and I've found out that a lot of things I'd never considered before we started swinging are a lot of fun. So, if the fellas want to see us girls playing, and the woman wants that too, I'll get in touch with my bisexual side and we'll let them watch while we enjoy ourselves.'

Marlon makes a comment here but it's spoken softly and Maria doesn't respond. 'I don't do anal sex,' she continues. 'I won't do anal sex. That part of my body was designed for things to come out – not go in. We had a couple round once who mentioned it, and she said anal sex was better than vaginal penetration, but even if it is, I'm not going to try it. She let us watch while her partner penetrated her anus. And I have to admit, she did look like she enjoyed it more than proper penetration. But it was going in her anus and I was thinking, *That can't be right.* I know my boundaries and that's one thing I've never done and I'm never going to do. Marlon knows and respects that – he doesn't think it's natural either – so I can't say I'm ever likely to try anal sex.

'I also don't like stuff involving pain or pee. Those things don't seem necessary. Where's the fun in peeing? And, if you're meeting a couple for pleasure, what's the point of having pain instead? That just seems daft to me. And why bring in pain and pee, and anal sex, when there are so many fun things you can do together as a couple that are genuinely pleasurable?' She pauses and waits, in case Marlon or myself have an answer to her question. Before the expectant silence can become uncomfortable, she waves this subject aside with another flutter of her hands. 'We've been at ours with a couple one week, all four of us having good, healthy sex together. We've had the porn video playing behind us and all of us have been doing something that is exciting and fun, pleasurable and different. And then, a week later, we'll be in the same place with another couple and we'll be doing something completely different from the previous week but it's just as sexy and just as much fun and it's all pleasure without any pain.

'But we always stay in the same room. All four of us together. There are so many things you can do in a room together when there's four of you. And, as stupid as this probably sounds, I'd feel as though I was cheating on Marlon if he wasn't in the room with me.'

Nadine and Nigel are in their late thirties. The couple both work in publishing. Nadine has one young child from a previous relationship and he spends his weekends with his biological father. Nadine and Nigel live in Kent and have been swinging for six years.

Nadine: 'The first time Nigel and I met up with a couple we all four shared the same room. It was a good night. I hated it. It wasn't really the first time we'd tried swinging.'

Nadine talks in a manner that is probably kindest described as caffeinated. When the contradiction of her statements is pointed out she grins, shakes her head and takes a deep breath to begin again. 'We'd talked around the subject and decided to give it a go a year earlier but never got close to managing anything. We'd posted an ad on the net, it was Swing-Swing, but the replies didn't do anything for me. The couples I liked were the ones that Nigel said were so-so. The ones he liked were the ones that I thought were bleargh. Which meant a few more months of saucy conversations and verbal foreplay as we tried to work out what we wanted from a swinging couple. Our first shortlist said simply that they both had to be good-looking, he had to have a big cock, and she needed tits like beach balls. Then we stopped being stupid, started trying to be rational about the whole thing and maturely decided looks weren't important.

'A year went by from us saying, "Let's try it," and posting our ad on Swing-Swing. When the membership came up for renewal I thought, If we don't do something about this soon, we're never going to do it. I checked with Nigel, made sure he was serious about wanting to try it, and then I renewed the membership and called the first couple to respond to our new ad.'

Nadine laughs politely when it's pointed out that her response is surprisingly quick for someone from the publishing industry. She continues quickly, before the interruption can disturb her express train of thought. 'I used one of the pictures that Nigel had taken of me with his new digital camera. I was sitting on a chair in the Christine Keeler pose, bare legs over the sides and the back of the chair covering my snatch. I was leaning over the chair so that you could see a glimpse of nipple. And I'd combed my fringe and hung my head so you couldn't see my face. It looked good. It was under the caption *"First Time Couple Seek Education"*, or something clever like that.' Nadine tries to call the picture up on her laptop but it's not in the folder where she thought it would be. 'We had a response by the end of the day,' she continues. 'I called the first couple who met the age requirement. We'd stated no older than mid-thirties – I'm not into gerontophilia – and organised a meeting for the weekend. Nigel was a bit shocked that I'd done everything so quickly, and without consulting him. But he was fairly impressed with the picture the couple had sent through. They were a long way from being Ken and Barbie, but they were equally far from being Shrek and Fiona.'

This is a photograph Nadine *is* able to find and she shows me a picture of a naked couple, posing awkwardly for their picture, arms supportively wrapped behind each other's back.

'The rest of the week was a horny blur. I was feeling quite pleased with myself for organising things so efficiently. Nigel was constantly hard and we were at it three or four times a night, saying that we would do this, insisting we would try that and adamant we would do the other. It's not surprising that, with so much of a build-up, the eventual evening was a disappointment.

'We met them at a motel. Well, we met them at the restaurant next door to the motel. My ex had our son for the weekend. My mother was calling round at the house to feed the cat. And the weekend was ours. I'd dressed smart but sexy – black Wonderbra and matching thong – and Nigel looked very hot in his Diesels and a Lacoste shirt, and we sat in the restaurant waiting for our Ken and Barbie to arrive.

'They were prompt, five minutes early, and they were very pleasant. We had a light snack and a couple of glasses of wine and the conversation was going very easy. When we started chatting about sex, and our likes and dislikes, the compatibility seemed even better. I was getting quite excited by the idea that we might all soon be naked and I was really relieved when Nigel said, "Should we go back to our room to talk some more?"

'Ken pretended to look disappointed and said, "Are we only going to talk?" And Barbie giggled as though it was the Edinburgh comedy festival.' Nadine checks herself with a sour grin. 'That's just me being bitchy,' she explains. 'He was a fun guy and he had us all laughing as we went back to the motel and collapsed in the room.

'There was one double bed, a settee and a shelf for the kettle. The shower and loo were just behind the door in their separate en suite. Nigel had linked arms with Barbie to walk back to the room so I fell alongside Ken. His arm was around my waist with his hand on my bum and he kept leaning close to whisper questions about what I fancied doing. It was all very arousing.

'And the night did turn out to be a good one. Both of the boys wanted to watch me and Barbie going at it, so we stripped off and got down to it. It was my first bisexual experience and I thought it was intense. I'd always wondered what it would be like to kiss another woman, squeeze boobs that weren't mine and finger a pussy. And it was very exciting. I didn't feel any mental connection with Barbie – that name suits her pretty well because she was blonde and plastic – but she got me very wet and she did things with her tongue that Nigel has never – well, no man has ever – been able to do.'

When asked to clarify what Barbie had done, Nadine flushes slightly and shakes her head. 'She was just very good at oral sex. She managed to touch the right places. Get deeper when I wanted it. Go gently when I wanted that. And she managed it all without me having to tell her she was doing it wrong or needed to be doing it differently. Barbie made me come quite quickly. I wanted to make her come but I was getting nervous, it was my first time with a woman, and the distraction of being on the edge of orgasm and so perpetually excited messed with my concentration. I could see that Nigel and Ken were getting naked, both of them hard and watching us with these big leery grins plastered on their faces, and that was a little off-putting too. I remained very aroused. It was very sexy and intense. But I think, even then, I wasn't comfortable with being watched.' Nadine shrugs and the gesture seems to say, *That was how it happened: there's nothing I can do to rectify the situation now*. 'Barbie pulled herself away from me. She was kind about it but I could see she was a little sad that she hadn't had her climax. She gave me a kiss and said thanks and then glanced at the boys and said, "I need some cock. Who's going to oblige me?"

'Nigel obliged her and Ken came over to me and asked if I needed any cock. He was quite a decent size with a kink in the shaft that made it bend to the left. When he was inside me I knew I was being fucked by a different cock from Nigel's because it was larger and felt so different.

'And it should have been a good night. It was a good night. The bed was rocking from all four of us riding each other so vigorously. Barbie made these cute squeals every time Nigel thrust into her –' Nadine mimics this sound with 'eek! eek! eek!' noises '– and the whole room stank of sex and sweat in a dirty but good way. Ken was very capable and I should have been enjoying myself. But I couldn't quite get to a second climax.

'There was one point where all three of them fell on me and tried to make me come. Barbie was kissing me. Ken sucked on my left boob while Nigel went at my right. I had my eyes closed so I don't know whose fingers were pushing into my pussy. There were hands and mouths all over me and it really was the most turned on I'd ever been. It was like being in the middle of an orgy. But it still wasn't enough to make me come.

'I left the boys servicing Barbie for a second time on the bed while I sat on the settee and fingered myself to climax. When I did come I screamed. And I felt sore down there for hours afterwards. Three or four hours had gone past since we started and we were all exhausted. Ken and Barbie said goodnight and promised to get back in touch. And me and Nigel crashed out on the bed.

'We talked about it the next day and I told him I'd loved it and hated it. It had certainly been an experience. But something about the whole episode had stopped me from enjoying it properly. When I thought about it seriously I realised it was the fact that there were four of us in the room. It was too many of us. Certainly more than I could relax with. Nigel wanted to know if I'd do it again and I said I wanted to, but I didn't want to just sit there and wank as though I was watching live porn.'

Nadine pauses and collects her thoughts before carrying on. After the frantic speed of her speech before, the silence is surprisingly intense. 'The good thing about the conversation was that we were able to talk about it,' she admits. 'I'd thought I might be jealous, or Nigel might have had problems with the fact that I'd had sex with someone else. None of that seemed to be an issue and that was one of the things that amazed me. I left my first husband because I discovered he'd had an affair. I'd worried that I might be like that with Nigel once I'd seen him going with another woman. But there was no jealousy or anything. We were able to talk about the evening like sensible adults and we got excited about what had happened and looked forward to the next one. When we talked it through properly we both thought I would get more out of it if we went for different rooms.

'So I went back to Swing-Swing, got in touch with one couple who looked fairly decent, and we agreed to book adjacent rooms in the motel. The weekend went pretty much like the first time. We met in the same restaurant, chatted and got on well. And then we all decided it was time to go back to the rooms. I'd thought we would pair off straight away but, for some reason, we all ended up in my room and, because the lads wanted to see us girls playing together – and I have to admit the girl from this couple was gorgeous and I did want to play with her a little myself – it started off pretty much as our first night had done.

'This time though, our second time of swinging, I felt more comfortable having a naked woman underneath me and I managed to get more out of the experience. I think she was more attractive than Barbie, I certainly found her more mentally stimulating. She wasn't as empty-headed as Barbie had been. And we both brought each other off while the lads watched and gave encouraging comments. Instead of being scared, or whatever it was that had put me off my stride the first time, I felt in control and relaxed.

'She came to her climax while I was fingering her. It was unreal to watch a woman have an orgasm with my fingers inside her pussy. She looked all sweaty and dishevelled after and I figured I looked just as badly used. But none of us seemed to mind.

'She asked, "Are the boys going to join in now?"

'And I said, "You can stay here with Nigel. I'll take your guy next door with me." Then we each kissed our partners goodnight, and I took her boyfriend back to Nigel's room. It was a much better experience. Much more satisfying.

Nigel wasn't there, watching me, grinning at me and constantly checking that I was OK. And I was able to relax as I got screwed by the stranger who had just watched me licking and fingering his girlfriend. We were able to explore each other's bodies and do that in ways that I wouldn't have wanted if Nigel had been there watching.

'Again, my boy was with his biological father. My mother was feeding the cat. So we had the entire weekend at our disposal if we wanted. I settled in for a night of good satisfying rigorous sex, and I enjoyed every second of it.

'My mobile rang while I was still getting screwed. It was Nigel, asking if I was OK, and did I want him? I said, "Come here in ten minutes. I'll be ready for another cock then." It was surreal to be talking to him while I had another man's cock inside me. That was strange enough to make me desperate to come. We spent the night calling each other, Nigel coming back to me first as the other guy went back to his girlfriend. Then they called again and asked if we were ready to sleep or still wanting to play. I sent Nigel back to their room, and the boyfriend came back to me. And after that the girlfriend came in to see me while Nigel and the boyfriend stayed in their room and shared a bottle of wine while they chatted about women and stuff.' She flashes a devilish grin and adds, 'Or at least, that's what Nigel said they did.

'Looking back on it, I dread to think what the motel's staff have made of the security tapes. We weren't bothering to put clothes on to go to each other's rooms. It was never more than a quick scan outside the door to make sure the corridor was empty, and then popping out, knocking three times, and rushing into the other couple's room.

'But that has to be the only down side. Since then we've met up with one or two couples every month. It doesn't always work out. Sometimes pictures are misleading and some people photograph well but they're incredible munters in real life. But it's an exciting way to spend a weekend and it's something that has rejuvenated our sex life. Now that we've found the proper way to do it, swinging in separate rooms, we're pretty sure it's the best way for us.'

Olive is sixty-two and has been swinging for fourteen years. A retired teacher, with three adult children, she has been married to Oswald for thirty-eight years. The couple live in Stafford and regularly swap partners but they only ever indulge in separate-room swaps.

Olive: 'We get together between five and ten times a year. It's more of a social gathering than swinging per se. But it's always an enjoyable evening and the purpose of the evening does seem to be to get each guest into bed with someone other than their husband or wife.' Olive holds herself with so much poise and dignity she could pass for being a member of the royal family. 'We gather at Arnold's,' she explains. She refers to Arnold as though he is so well known he needs no surname for further identification. 'He has the largest house and has always hosted these soirees. For a while he sent out formal invitations, embossed lettering on cream vellum, but I think he was only doing that to show off that he'd bought a printing firm. One of the invitations said "knickers optional" which was vulgar but amusing. Nowadays he'll usually send an email or a text message, a month in advance, asking us to RSVP.

'Arnold's married to April. They celebrated their twenty-fifth last year but that party was open to children and grandchildren so nothing out of the ordinary occurred there. We don't have sex every time we visit Arnold and April. Only when they're hosting one of their parties. I think there have probably been about eighteen to twenty couples involved over the years, although there's rarely more than half a dozen couples turn up on any given occasion nowadays.

'Some of the couples tried it once and didn't seem to like it. I suppose it's not something that everyone cares to do, although I personally think that attitude is small-minded.' Olive wrinkles her nose in distaste as she says this. 'The numbers are sometimes low because not everyone can make every party that Arnold hosts. And, of course, the Grim Reaper has pruned our numbers over the years. But five or six couples are more than enough to make for a very interesting night and it's very rare that we come away disappointed. I can't recall ever coming away from Arnold's and thinking, "Well, I didn't enjoy that!" And I've never come out of a party and told Oswald, "That's the last time we're going to Arnold's." Even when it's not constant passion and orgasms, it's still a very exciting experience.' She adds that she has seen some couples leaving Arnold's parties and vowing never to return, but she dismisses these reactions as being from people who 'read tabloids and watch Jerry Springer'.

'The invitations, when they were printed, said we were expected at eight. The parties have always started at the same time, which is another of the reasons I always thought Arnold was being pretentious printing them in such an ostentatious way. Arnold lives about an hour away from us so it means setting off at seven, earlier if the traffic threatens to be difficult. We arrive, Arnold serves a glass of wine, sherry or port – whatever he's picked up cheapest from Lidl, I suppose – and then, around eight-thirty, April invites us through to the dining room for our dinner. It's rare to have any new blood join us nowadays, although I'd say it still happens maybe once a year. We're a very discreet group and it's not like we advertise for other couples to come and fill out the numbers.

'After the meal, Arnold walks around the table with a big glass bowl, encouraging the men to put their car keys in. It's an old feature of the parties that's remained over the years, even though it's a terrible anachronism. I'm the one who always drives us to the parties, and I think that a lot of the women who attend are drivers too. But because it's a tradition, all the men put their keys in before we retire for drinks in the drawing room.

'April is usually there, with sherry for the ladies and cognac for the gentlemen, and that's where Arnold joins us: with his bowl of car keys. He'll walk amongst us, offering the bowl to all the ladies, and we each pick a random set of keys. Then it's a matter of mingling with everyone and finding out who you're going to be fucking that night.'

Olive enunciates the expletive with the exquisite pronunciation of someone who fared very well in elocution lessons. It sounds strange to hear the word being produced so correctly.

'I have to say that part of the evening is where my excitement starts to rise. Holding a strange set of car keys is almost like foreplay for me. I can't rent a car from Avis without feeling a little giddy when they hand over the keys, and I know that response is all down to Arnold's parties.

'Once I've mingled and found the rightful owner of the keys, I usually say something polite like, "Oh! Lucky me!" and then I'll find Oswald, give him a parting kiss, and tell him I'll see him in the morning.

'That's one of our traditions. I don't think all the other couples who attend Arnold's do that. I do it mainly to remind Oswald that I love him, and I'll be thinking about him while I'm with another man, and also to find out whom he'll be with.

'There's very seldom any visible signs of swapping or swinging in the drawing room. Early on in the history of our parties a couple of the women tried to appear shocking and independent by getting their boobs out or stripping naked. One woman insisted on giving her husband's cock a goodnight kiss before she went off with Oswald. And she then proceeded to fellate him to the point of ejaculation while the rest of us stood around sipping amontillado. Oswald won't hear me say a word against that trollop, but I thought her behaviour was unseemly and brazen. I was pleased to see that Arnold stopped inviting her after that party. I much prefer the company of more sophisticated ladies and gentlemen who know what's going to happen in the evening, and don't feel the need to make a big demonstration about their open understanding of sex and sexuality.

'But, that aside, once I've discovered the owner of the keys there will generally be a half-hour's polite conversation that can become suggestive and arousing. After half an hour most of the people in the room are ready to try and slip subtly out of the drawing room and go upstairs to one of the many bedrooms in Arnold's house.

'Getting out of the room without being noticed is something of a fine art. If someone notices a couple trying to slip away, there'll be a loud cheer around the room and the embarrassment is crushing. My favourite trick is to tell my partner for the evening that I'm going to visit the lavatory, and suggest he join me upstairs in five minutes. It's a sly old ploy but it's not failed me in the last decade.' Her expression at this clever device is one of sly satisfaction. 'I don't feel as though I'm being used. It doesn't matter to me that I have no say in who I'll be sleeping with. The random element, picking out keys from a bowl, makes everything so much more exciting. If I was given a choice, and had to go round the table thinking, do I want this man or that man, the whole thing would be horribly embarrassing. How could I pick one of my friends over the other? What criterion could I possibly use to weigh the advantages and disadvantages of this man against that man? The random selection cuts out all that process and I don't think it has any faults, except for the one time I accidentally ended up with Oswald's car keys.'

Olive gives a stately nod when asked a question and says, 'Yes, it has happened that I've ended up in the company of someone that I didn't find particularly attractive or desirable. But not every lottery ticket is a winner. And, although I might not like the look of one individual, I have no idea what he's going to be like in bed. The chances are, if I didn't have an immediate attraction to him, he's going to provide something I wouldn't ordinarily have experienced.

'And isn't that the point of these parties?

'As an example, about five years ago, I ended up with a rather uncouth man who was attending his second or third party. Usually Oswald and I try to get to know everyone at Arnold's but this man had been difficult to talk to and his trophy wife was equally aloof. When I found I had his key in my hand I did think about feigning illness and getting Oswald to take me home. That thought seemed like a necessity when my uncouth partner for the evening slapped a hand on my backside, clutched one buttock tight and bellowed, "This is a nice piece of arse I'll be fucking tonight."

'But, instead of pretending to be ill, I simply smiled at him and said it was more than a nice piece of arse. And we laughed together. When we got in the bedroom, his lack of manners and etiquette became immaterial. He had no social skills for the party downstairs but he was extremely competent in bed. He had the stamina to go on and on, he had a surprisingly powerful physique, and his uncouth vocabulary was incredibly arousing.

' "Do you like fucking my big cock?" he demanded. "Do you want my big cock up your tight little arse? Do you want to take my cock in your mouth and swallow my spunk? Do you want me to spunk up your arse?" '

Again, Olive's perfect pronunciation of these vulgarities makes them sound strange and unfamiliar.

'He was so vigorous and good at what he was doing that I didn't mind where he did it or how. I told him as much and he called me "a randy old bird". After the gentle sex I was used to from so many of the others who attend Arnold's parties, he was a breath of fresh air. He treated his sex far more seriously than any of the other men I'd ever been with and I have to admit it was far more satisfying. But that was a man who, if I'd been given the choice instead of randomly selecting car keys, I would never have picked in a million years.

'It's fair to say that every party is different. Even if you end up with a partner you've been with before, the experience will always be something different. Oswald and I have found the parties enhance our sex life in ways I would never have imagined. I've found scratch marks on his back after parties, and been highly aroused by the idea of who put them there and what might have been happening at the time. I came back from one party with a love-bite on my bottom. Oswald got very aroused every time he saw that. And, when we tell each other about how we spent the evening, it rekindles the initial arousal as we share the details. I suppose it's a way for us to talk openly and honestly about sex, excite each other, and constantly keep the topic fresh.

'Arnold's parties, although he makes them a little pompous, are always entertaining and I wouldn't want to miss one for the world. Obviously we've had to decline a few invitations over the years. Family commitments take priority and Arnold has been known to organise parties during the summer, when a lot of us are away. But, if it's at all possible that we can be there, Oswald and I will usually make the effort.'

Olive sits back in her chair and takes the opportunity to ask if there are any more questions. Although she has been the interviewee, there has never been any doubt about which one of us was in control of the conversation. 'We've been visiting Arnold's for almost fifteen years now,' she explains. 'And we're very close friends with many of his regular guests. I won't say the fact we've had sex with them is incidental. We would never have met them if we hadn't all been of a mind to humour Arnold and his initial desire to host a swinging party, so the sex played an important part somewhere along the line. But the sex isn't the most important part of the arrangement. For me, the parties provide something I can't seem to find anywhere else – they give me an opportunity to feel young and desirable. I've tried cosmetic surgery in many forms, as well as every skin-rejuvenating product on the market, and I can honestly say Arnold's parties are the only thing that consistently makes me feel young.'

DISCRETION ASSURED

> **Broad-minded Couple 28f 35m**
> (Cambridge area) seek same for adult fun.
> Open to anything as long as it's fun and
> discreet. P.O. Box AL006

The risk of exposure is a very real and dangerous threat to swingers and the need for secrecy can be imperative. The swinging lifestyle is not one that is readily understood or accepted by outsiders. Gossip and rumours alone can cause a swinging couple severe distress; stories that are substantiated with facts can make private details scandalously public. Many of the ex-swingers I spoke with had given up their involvement in the lifestyle because the secrecy of their activities had been compromised or they perceived a very real danger that personal details could be exposed.

Whilst writing this book I have spoken with ex-swingers who have been forced to change jobs and move homes because their involvement in the lifestyle had become known to a third party. One American lady explained that her single venture into swinging had ended with embarrassing pictures being distributed at the school where she worked. This forced her to change careers, move out of the state, and rebuild her life from scratch. Others, not quite so unfortunate, have confided that swinging was directly responsible for a permanent and damaging rift between themselves and members of their immediate family.

However, even though this danger is always present, singles and couples continue to swing and there are some who seem unconcerned by the potential consequences. The majority of active swingers tend to avoid the risk of scandal and ostracism by simply guarding the secrets of their private lives. But there are others who simply refuse to consider it as a potential problem.

'If people find out what we're doing and they don't like it,' one Hampshire couple explained, 'then that's their problem: not ours.' A lady in Yorkshire added, 'My mother knows that I swing. She doesn't approve but, since I'm in my thirties and have been married for seven years, it's not like her approval matters.'

However, while many swingers took similar defiant stances, there were many more who did admit that there would always be someone whom they wouldn't tell about their private life. And a large majority of swingers admitted the one thing that they didn't like about swinging was the fear of being caught.

The following interviews concentrated on the problems that are associated with swinging in relation to the risks of exposure and the consequential dangers of being discovered. As is the case with all the interviews conducted for this book, the subject details have been changed to protect identities.

Penny is thirty-nine and used to be an enthusiastic advocate of dogging. She is tall, dark-haired and describes herself as a curvy size 12. The mother of two children, she lives with Peter in Leicestershire and works part-time at a local cafeteria.

Penny: 'I used to enjoy dogging. I like dogging. There's an atmosphere to dogging that you can't get anywhere else. We've tried the parties and the swapping stuff but none of it has the same feel as you get from dogging. There's a buzz to the whole thing that's impossible to describe. I like it for several reasons. I like the fact that I'm usually the centre of attention. I like the fact that it's outdoors and so it's almost semi-public – like exhibitionism. And I like the fact that I can pretty much do whatever I want.' The enthusiasm on her face as she speaks about this subject suggests that Penny doesn't simply like dogging – she loves dogging.

'The places we visited were always fairly busy. Peter would get the details from a place online and we seldom had to travel more than twenty miles to find a particular site. There'd be a few cars there when we arrived. And Peter was always happy for the evening to end up with me naked on the backseat and blowing random cocks through the windows.

'It could get really bold and daring. I seldom went with the idea of having sex. I never went with more than an idea of blowing a guy or three and flashing my boobs or my quim. That's always enough to get me wet. But there were times when I was up for it and, if Peter had already come inside me, I often needed another cock or two to finish me off. On those nights it could turn into quite an event, if we let it. And, after those nights, I always came back home satisfied and looking forward to our next dogging adventure.'

Penny's enthusiastic smile fades as she says, 'But we stopped about six months ago and we haven't done it since. It had been the usual sort of evening. I'd been naked when we set off, just wearing a coat to cover myself, and Peter had plugged the location into the TomTom. We got there about an hour after nightfall and there were already a couple of cars waiting. I could see a woman on her knees behind a Renault, sucking a guy while two blokes nearby had their pants round their ankles while they wanked for her. It was really hot and horny stuff.

'Peter told me to unfasten my coat but I was well ahead of him. Even as he was saying the words I was rolling my coat up and putting it safe under the seat.' Penny's seriousness disappears beneath an expression of good-humoured forbearance as she explains, 'Past experience has taught us to be careful with things like that. You can't leave anything visible in the car because there's a danger it could go missing. Peter locked the TomTom in the glove compartment. The only thing on the dashboard was a half-empty bottle of diet Pepsi. If you don't hide everything some thieving shit will steal it.' Brushing this detail aside she says, 'But that's only a minor inconvenience. If you don't leave anything out in the open, there's less risk of it being stolen.

'So, that evening, Peter flicked on the car's interior light, and then started sucking my breasts. I stared out of the window and watched the doggers looking our way and started to get the familiar thrill that comes from dogging.'

Penny's comments lead to a discussion on how to properly name those people who participate in dogging. Penny insists that she and her husband could never be described as 'doggers' as that's a term that only applies to the men who congregate at dogging sites with the intention of getting off with a 'dogging couple'. It seems like a suitable way of clarifying the distinction and Penny continues to explain what happened on her last night of dogging.

'They didn't all come running over. The guy who was getting blown by the blonde behind the Renault didn't even look at us. Neither did either of the guys who were jerking off as they watched the blonde swallow their pal. But we'd caught a few interested glances as we were driving into the park and within a couple of minutes of Peter starting to suck on my boobs we had a half-dozen or so blokes grinning through the windscreen and the side windows and watching what we were up to. Then the tapping on the window started.'

Penny explains that this is common practice at dogging sites. What would seem rude and intrusive under other circumstances is acceptable and expected in dogging.

'I wound the window down,' she explains, 'and glanced at the guy peering through. He was in his late twenties or early thirties, wearing a tracksuit and grinning. He told me I had nice tits and I wound the window down more and asked, "Do you want to touch them?" And that was all it took to get us started that evening. My head was on the same level as his waist. I could see the bulge at the front of his jogging pants. And when he reached in to start fumbling with my tits I was able to stroke his cock through his joggers. Once Peter had me warmed up – and it didn't take him long to get me warmed up – I was in a mood to take the guy's cock out of his pants and suck him for a while.' She smiles sadly and confides, 'That was really horny. Some of these doggers see so little action that, when you just take their cocks in your mouth without them having to beg, they're stupidly grateful. And, like I said, it worked out to be a pretty good night.'

Penny pauses to collect her thoughts before explaining the specific way she and Peter enjoy their dogging. 'I usually stay in the car. I don't like going out in the cold and, when you're starkers at a dogging site, it really can get cold. I crawled over to the backseat eventually and got myself on all fours. With the rear doors open I had one guy leaning in and kissing my face while two blokes behind me were reaching inside to finger my quim. One of them kept trying to shove his thumb up my arse but I told him I wasn't doing any kinky stuff and so he stopped. Peter joined me in the backseat when my excitement really kicked in and he fucked me doggy-style while I had my head through the window and sucked two cocks at the same time. That was probably the most unusual thing about the evening up to then. A lot of guys don't like you to blow them at the same time as you're blowing someone else. Even though a woman is sucking them, I think they're scared there is something gay about having their cock so close to another man's. But neither of these guys seemed troubled by that. They were both hard and tasty and I sucked on them as Peter gave me a good hard fucking from behind. I told him I was swallowing come while he fucked me and that triggered off his climax. And, while it felt good to have him pump his load inside me, it didn't properly get me off. So I said, the first guy to slap a condom on his cock could get sloppy seconds. The next thing I knew a guy was pushing his cock into me and I was getting fucked hard by a complete stranger.'

Penny grins shyly and adds, 'Needless to say, I came. Being screwed by a stranger, a man I hadn't seen and didn't know, was a real thrill. All that I knew about him was that his hands were cold and his cock was hard and inside me. Even now I get turned on remembering that moment. Back then it was enough to make me come hard and quick.' She wriggles in her seat and fans her chest for a moment before continuing. 'Once I've come I can't stand being touched. I get very sensitive on my way up to an orgasm and, once that's happened, I can't take any more. My quim gets hypersensitive and I can't have anyone touch me there or on my breasts. Peter knows what I'm like so he helped push everyone away and told them all I was having a break. I got back into the passenger seat and had a fag with my coat wrapped round my shoulders. The bottle of diet Pepsi was still on the dashboard so I had a drink of that to take the taste of cock out of my mouth. Our usual routine is, once I've come, we wait for half an hour. If I feel up for another session, we'll go for it. If I'm not in the mood, we'll drive home.

'And I can't honestly say which way it was going to go that evening. I'd enjoyed it and I might have wanted more. But the orgasm had been strong and satisfying and if I was going to have another that evening I wanted it to be with Peter. I'd got the window wound down so the cigarette smoke didn't fill up the car. The guys who had been round our car were going back into the shadows. The blonde with the Renault was long gone but there was a Citroën on the other side of the park and their interior light was on and, because nothing was happening at our car, everyone seemed to be flocking in that direction. I could also see another car light further away from us, so there were other attractions for the doggers to enjoy. Peter had just asked me if I was up for seconds and I was trying to decide how to answer when I heard someone outside the car say, "Is that Penny?"

She shivers and says, 'That sent me cold. I don't go out of my way to disguise my appearance when we go dogging. We travel about twenty miles away from our home address, it's always dark and I figure that people aren't really bothered about my face. But I never thought I'd be recognised by someone. I threw away my cigarette, told Peter I wanted to go home, straight away, and we shot out of there.' She sighs and adds, 'It wouldn't have troubled me so much if we hadn't been followed. I think, if we hadn't been followed, I might have decided to do it again. Obviously it would have been at a different location, but I wouldn't have called an end to the dogging that night. But being followed really freaked me out.

'I was watching in the wing mirror after we'd pulled out of the car park and I saw another car coming out moments after we'd left. I was watching through the rear window and the car seemed to be behind us forever. I told Peter that I thought we were being followed. It sounded like something out of a spy movie and I expected him to laugh at me and say I was being stupid. Instead he put his foot down and started trying to lose our tail.'

Penny shrugs and says, 'It should have been exciting. But I was just cold, frightened and scared. The car stayed behind us for about twenty minutes. Peter kept turning into different roads once we hit the town, but it kept following. I was racking my brains to try and remember if I'd seen anyone I knew at the dogging park but it had been dark and I hadn't really been looking at faces. I was worried that it was someone I knew from work, the café gets fairly busy and there are a lot of customers as well as staff. I started panicking that they were following us home. I was worried that we'd just picked up a stalker or some sort of psychopath.' She's frowning as she says, 'It really was nerve-racking.

'Peter pulled over in a lay-by where there was a police car and pretended he was lost and looking for directions. The car that had been following us went past. I didn't recognise the car and I couldn't see much about the person behind the wheel other than to see it was a man. We waited half an hour before driving off and Peter took the long route back home, with me constantly watching out of the rear window in case the car appeared again.'

Bitterly, Penny says, 'We haven't been dogging since. I'll be honest and admit that I miss it. Dogging is a fun and unique way for a woman to enjoy herself. Where else can a woman go and be treated like a slut and, at the same time, boss men around and tell them that she wants this cock but she doesn't want that one? I desperately want to go back and experience it again. But I'm not going to do it until I'm one hundred per cent sure I won't be recognised or followed. We've talked about maybe travelling further out to go dogging, which is one option, or me wearing sunglasses or a wig, or Peter getting a different car. But it all seems so excessive and over the top for something that's supposed to be impulsive and spontaneous. So, at the moment, dogging is something we can't do because I can't risk being found out or followed again. But one day, and one day soon I hope, I will get back out to the dogging sites.'

Kylie is thirty-eight years old and lives in the Midlands. Five feet eight, with blonde hair and blue eyes, she attributes her physique to her work as a health and fitness instructor. Kylie has been married to Shaun for eighteen years and the couple have been swinging for four years. They like to experiment with different ways of swinging and have tried soft-swaps, full swaps, threesomes and dogging.

Kylie: 'I'm surprised we ever got into swinging. The first time we'd arranged to meet a couple was like something out of a French farce. We'd told them we'd meet them at a local pub. We'd exchanged pictures and details on the net, and we got ourselves excited and worked up ready to meet them. Then we turned up at the pub. And my brother-in-law and his wife were there.'

There are five of us sitting around the restaurant table as Kylie talks. It's late on a Saturday afternoon, Kylie and Shaun had arranged to meet another swinging couple after our interview, but traffic delays have brought all five of us together at the same time. Kylie assures me she is comfortable answering questions in front of the other couple and explains this is not the first time they've seen them. On the subject of encountering her brother-in-law and his wife on their first attempt at swinging, she says, 'It was awkward and embarrassing to say the least. The couple we were meeting knew us by our handles from the chatrooms: Jack and Jill. We knew them as Charles and Camilla. That meant, when we were trying to get away from Shaun's brother, we were fumbling for how to explain who our friends were, and what they were called, and panicking in case Charles and Camilla came over to the bar and shouted, "Hi! It's Jack and Jill, isn't it? We recognise you from the nuddy pictures you sent us. Are we still on for that foursome tonight?"'

Everyone at the table laughs and the sound is loud enough to draw attention from other diners. Kylie blushes from the attention.

'We've found out since that no swinging couple is so tactless,' she admits. Glancing at the other couple she cheekily adds, 'Well, not many of them are. But at the time, in those few minutes, it was a major worry. It was one of those horrifying experiences that made me wonder what I was getting myself into. If it had worked out differently, I think we would have stopped swinging before we'd even started. Luckily Charles and Camilla were experienced swingers. They saw we were chatting with someone, nodded politely in our direction and took a table near the door. I think they'd been able to work out what was happening from the horrified panic they could see on my face. Shaun's mobile beeped a couple of minutes later and it was a text message from Charles and Camilla asking us if we wanted to meet somewhere else. Shaun left me with his brother, discreetly went over and introduced himself to Charles and Camilla and explained what had happened. Then he called me over to meet a couple of his "friends" from the office. I said goodnight to Shaun's brother, and we were able to get away from them without too many awkward questions.'

Shaun adds that it had also been nerve-racking for him.

Their friends confirm that they have experienced similar close calls.

'That evening worked out quite well for us,' Kylie continues. 'We'd told Charles and Camilla we were new to swinging and wanted to take things slowly. They came back to ours and we had our first experience of soft-swinging. We were each with our respective partners, kissing, cuddling and getting intimate, but watching each other too. Camilla had a gorgeous body and looked really sexy in a crotchless body-stocking. Charles was in pretty good shape. Camilla stripped down to her body-stocking and started using her mouth on her husband's erection. Shaun was getting very excited by all of this, as was I, and we stripped down as well. Before any of us had sex, before it got as far as proper penetration in front of another couple, Charles asked if we wanted to swap for a single kiss.'

Kylie glances at the other couple when she says this and gives the impression that our fellow diners might conceal their identities under the names Charles and Camilla.

'That was exciting,' Kylie admits. 'I was naked and kissing a naked man. My husband was naked and kissing a near-naked woman. The thrill that I got from that was the thing that I'd fantasised about most when we'd talked about swinging. I don't know if I wanted things to go further with them that evening. I wasn't being shy about stroking Charles's erection when we kissed. But Charles pulled away and said, with it being our first time, we should take things slowly and stick to what we'd agreed. We've seen them since, a couple of times, and gone on to enjoy a full swap. They're a lovely couple – attractive and considerate – and the ideal pair for introducing newbies to swinging.'

It's tempting to glance at the other couple, and see if they're responding to the praise Kylie is heaping on Charles and Camilla. But it's more polite to concentrate on Kylie.

'The only problem with that evening had been the embarrassment of seeing my brother-in-law and his wife in the pub. While we'd been in the pub I'd been very self-conscious that Shaun's brother might be watching us. I'd been thinking all sorts of paranoid thoughts: that he would guess why we were there; and what we were planning to do with Charles and Camilla; and go on to blurt our secret to all and sundry. It was a very uncomfortable experience.' She glances at her husband for confirmation and says, 'Shaun said afterwards that, the next time we arranged to meet a couple, we had to do it somewhere different. That suited me because I didn't want to suffer that sort of embarrassment again but I did want to do more with the swinging. Our taster session with Charles and Camilla had given me an appetite for more.

'So, the next time we arranged to meet someone, Shaun suggested we go to a pub that was just on the outskirts of the town. It was one of those pubs with a restaurant next door to a motel. Close enough to the motorway to be convenient but far enough from home so we were unlikely to meet anyone we knew. We'd only gone there to use the pub and meet a man called Ricky. We were still interested in seeing other couples but I'd fantasised about having Shaun and another man at the same time. Ricky had done threesomes before and, through chatting to him online, he seemed like the perfect man to help us out. As it turned out, he was very good at what he did. But Shaun's sister came into the restaurant just as we were leaving.'

Her story is interrupted as the other couple express disbelief that Kylie and Shaun could encounter close relatives on their first two swinging experiences. Kylie agrees that the odds of it happening were phenomenal while Shaun promises them it most certainly did happen and almost caused them to give up swinging. Kylie also adds that the situation wasn't as bad as it could have been. 'It could have been far more embarrassing. Five minutes before we decided to leave I'd been French kissing Ricky while Shaun watched. We were sat in a discreet corner of the pub and Ricky had been able to touch my leg and more and get me very much in the mood for going home and shagging both of them. If Shaun's sister had seen that – with Shaun just sat there, sipping his wine and watching while I wrestled tongues with a handsome stranger – I doubt we would have been able to explain our way out of the situation. As it was, her appearance still came close to spoiling the evening for us. The three of us were walking out of the pub, me between Ricky and Shaun, both men with an arm around my waist, and Shaun's sister almost bumped into us as we met at the door.'

The husband of the other couple asks Kylie how they explained the situation to Shaun's sister.

'Shaun was the first to speak,' she tells him. 'He said Ricky was an old friend of mine from college. Ricky shook her hand and I saw his fingers were still wet from having been inside me five minutes earlier. Loose introductions were made and, although Shaun's sister invited us to stay for another drink, Ricky sensibly made an excuse and said he had to get back home. I told him I'd see him to his car, left Shaun to deal with his sister, and gave Ricky directions back to our house. He was waiting outside for us when we returned and he was playfully laughing about our obvious embarrassment at almost getting caught. I didn't mind his joking and it helped make the mood easier and friendlier when I started to strip for him and Shaun later that evening. Again, it was another good night. Ricky had asked us what we wanted when we chatted online but our plans had been clarified when we talked in the pub. I'd said I wanted to shag him while Shaun watched, then shag Shaun, and then shag both of them. Ricky had built on that and said it would be fun for all of us if the evening started with me doing a strip, then fucking him and then Shaun, and he got me all excited asking me to describe exactly how I wanted both men for the evening's climax. The sexy talk and fantasies, and then achieving those fantasies, had me very wet and very ready for them both.'

The conversation around the restaurant table moves on to more mundane matters as the waitress brings starters. Both couples seem extremely adept at disguising the fact that they have been indulging in verbal foreplay and it's almost like a natural extension of that skill when Kylie returns to her original point as soon as the waitress is out of earshot.

'There had been other meetings in the intervening period. A few of them had been frustrating no-shows. A couple of them had turned out to be fun nights and one of them had turned up but been such a big disappointment that nothing happened. But the thing I remember most about our first year in swinging was the number of times we came close to being found out. After seeing Shaun's sister at the restaurant, I suggested we should invite his mother to our next swinging meet. We both saw the funny side and continued trying to find places to meet other swingers that were supposed to be discreet. But it would happen that, around every third or fourth meet, we'd find ourselves cringing and saying, "Oh! No! What are they doing here?"'

Everyone around the table is laughing as Kylie explains, 'Shaun's brother appeared a second time, when we were meeting our first black couple. One of my supervisors from the gym was at the café where we had arranged to meet a single bi female. I've seen clients from the gym in some of the pubs and Shaun has seen business colleagues from work.'

The conversation around the table trails away from the interview. Shaun offers his opinions on the dangers of being discovered and the other couple have a lot of valid comments to make and recount similar anecdotes to those that Kylie has already offered. Kylie lets them talk while she samples her garlic mushrooms and then summarises her thoughts neatly as the others eat.

'I think I worried about it more in those first few years. Certainly those first few months. I was very worried that someone would find out what we were doing and then the gossip would begin. But that didn't happen and, because we've braved our way through the situation, it's meant we're known for having a broad social circle and that's been a very positive thing. We get invited to lots of non-swinging parties, simply because people think we're party animals and have to be invited if they're throwing a party. And we're much more relaxed about bumping into non-swinging friends and acquaintances when we hook up with other swingers. I seriously considered giving up on the swinging before it had properly begun. Shaun was of the same mind and we were both terrified that we were going to be at the centre of a huge scandal.' She smiles for all four of us before adding, 'But after four years of doing some pretty outrageous things, I'm awfully glad that we chose to continue.'

Rosie, an IT specialist based in the Peterborough area, is twenty-seven years old and lives with Robert. The couple have been together for three years and Rosie explains that their relationship has incorporated some element of swinging since very early on. Rosie and Robert have currently suspended their swinging while they try to start a family.

Rosie: 'At uni, the most erotic thing I came across was the story about Kelly, a girl who was in one of my classes. I remember it vividly, I think, because Kelly was one of the first girls I ever had a crush on. Kelly had got a boyfriend, I heard, and they were at it most nights – the way students are when they hook up together and are living in student accommodation away from home and off campus. They were sharing a communal house rent close to the uni with four other students. Kelly and her boyfriend were at it one night. They weren't being particularly quiet. And they'd left the bedroom door ajar.'

Rosie raises her eyebrows, suggesting it's obvious where this story is leading and why it had such a powerful impact. She continues excitedly, as though this old story still enthrals her. 'Kelly was laid on the bed. Her boyfriend was between her legs in a pretty conventional missionary position. And she noticed, over his shoulder, staring through the gap of the open door, was one of the other students who shared their house. If it had been me, I wouldn't have known what to do. I think I'd have screamed, or told him to fuck off, or called an end to everything then and there. But Kelly was more hard-faced than that. She carried on getting fucked by her boyfriend and told the guy at the door, "You can come in and watch, if you want. But you're not joining in."'

Rosie sits back and takes a deep breath. She looks flushed from telling the story, but not with embarrassment. 'I heard the story in the refectory halfway through term. I heard the story from one of the other girls who had the house share with Kelly, so I strongly believe it was true. And it was one of those stories that seemed to define all my future desires and fantasies. From then on, I wanted to be fucked like Kelly and have someone watching. I wanted to be the only woman with two lads. And I wanted to be in control.' She pauses and reflects for a moment before adding, 'Of course, I wouldn't have minded watching Kelly. She was a very self-consciously sexy young woman. She wore the most revealing and inappropriate clothes for lectures: ultra-minis, with tight-tight tops or bumster jeans with a balconette. And I did make a couple of attempts to get invited to the shared house in the hope that I'd be able to make something happen. Or at least see something. But nothing ever came of that.'

Rosie's resigned expression suggests she has suffered greater setbacks in her life, but few that fill her with such regret. 'I quickly realised Kelly was out of my league but I continued wanting to have what Kelly had experienced. I wanted to be with one partner and I wanted us to be watched. Whenever I talked with boyfriends about our mutual fantasies, that would be the first thing I'd say. Of course, most lads just want to see two women fucking, which I can understand. And I'd have been happy to get it on with another woman if they'd been able to introduce me to a likely candidate. But none of the lads I went with knew any amenable bisexual women. And none of them ever suggested that they had a friend who would be interested in watching us. Which is probably why most of those relationships fizzled away to nothing. It wasn't until I met Robert that I finally found a man who was comfortable with the idea of being watched during sex.'

Rosie pauses again and collates her thoughts carefully before continuing. She smiles when she talks about Robert and makes it clear that she considers him her soul mate. 'We met through my job. We dated for a couple of weeks, fucked a couple of times, and found we were fairly compatible. We'd become a steady item by the time we were discussing fantasies and we were comfortable enough with each other to be very honest. It was a Saturday night when I told him my fantasy was to be watched while we were fucking. I explained what I'd heard about my friend Kelly at uni and I told Robert how much that anecdote had affected me. He listened patiently and then asked if I wanted to be watched by a man or a woman.

'No one had ever asked me that question before and it got me really excited. I thought about it –' Rosie's flushed colouring suggests she thought about it in very explicit terms '– and told Robert I'd always liked the idea of being watched by a man although, now he'd suggested it, I thought the idea of being watched by a woman was equally arousing. He asked if I was serious and said his brother, Tom, would almost certainly be up for watching if I really wanted that to happen.

'I was so amazed I said yes straight away.

'Robert gave me a week to think about it and every night of that week we fucked while I was fantasising about what it would be like to have his brother watching us. It was incredible sex. Very passionate and very intense.' Bashfully, Rosie decides it was 'Some of the best I've ever had with just one other partner in the room. The next Friday night, six days after we'd originally talked about it, Robert asked me again if I was sure I wanted to go through with being watched and I told him I definitely wanted it to happen.

'We'd been fucking again, Robert has always known how to get me horny, and both of us were naked in the lounge of his flat. I told him that I still wanted to go through with it and he said that was a relief because Tom had been watching from the kitchen while we fucked for the last half-hour.'

Rosie is almost laughing as she nods excitedly. 'Robert called him in and his brother stepped through from the kitchen, grinning like an idiot and leering at my tits and pussy. It wasn't exactly the situation I'd wanted. But it was close enough and I appreciated the way Robert had planned everything. If he'd waited until the Saturday night I most likely would have backed out or made an excuse or something. But, making sure it was something I still wanted, and then surprising me with Tom being in the kitchen: that was just inspired. I sat next to Robert, smiling coolly up at Tom and trying to act dead casual. I asked Tom if he had enjoyed the show and he chuckled and said, "Oh! Yes." Then I asked him if he wanted to watch a repeat performance and his eyes lit up. He was practically drooling. Robert said it was going to take him a while to get hard again, and I could see what he was suggesting, but I didn't fancy that. I only wanted to be watched. So, I went down on Robert and sucked him hard again while his brother stood over us watching.

'Robert said he wouldn't object to Tom servicing me, if that was what I wanted, but I reminded him that having Tom service me had never been part of the deal. I told him that I only wanted someone watching us and I said I'd had a really exciting time while that was happening. I was waggling my bare ass in the air so Robert's brother could see my wet pussy. I was making a big show of sucking Robert's cock and getting him hard and rubbing him between my tits. When I eventually straddled Robert, I turned and stared his brother straight in the eye and said, "You can wank, if you want. But you're not fucking me."'

Rosie's expression is triumphant as she explains, 'In that moment, I felt just like Kelly. Of course, I fucked Tom before the end of the evening. The whole experience was so horny I couldn't have not fucked him. Tom was stroking this big erection, grinning at me and clearly wanting me, and I was getting off on the attention. When Robert came for a second time that night, I still needed more and I told Tom that he could fuck me if he made sure it was good.

'I think I had Robert three times that night and his brother twice. And that was what got us into swinging. I'd felt elated to experience the same thrill that Kelly must have had back at uni. By having a lad watch me while I fucked someone else, and then telling him what he could and couldn't do, I felt empowered. But also, by fucking Robert's brother, I'd learnt that two men can better satisfy a woman than a single man on his own.' Rosie's expression is earnest as she adds, 'I think women's bodies are built to be pleasured by more than one man. I think the happiest and most satisfied women are those who act on that knowledge.

'Of course I serviced Robert's brother a couple of times more after that. Usually it was the same script with him watching and wanking first while I said he wasn't going to fuck me. Then I'd give in and suck Tom back to life so he could bang me properly. Sometimes I'd suck Robert and Tom at the same time so they could do me together like I was a restaurant door – one of them sliding out as the other one pushed in. But all that time Robert and I were trawling the personals looking for single lads or couples with bi-curious females.'

Rosie purses her lips and says softly, 'Our secret was almost exposed when we visited Robert's brother for a meal. Tom's wife, Tina, was there and I thought she knew what Tom did when he came round to ours. I'd been looking forward to meeting her because I assumed she was open-minded and generous. I told Tina she was lucky to have such a capable husband and she gave me one of those puzzled looks that I should have understood straight away. Thinking back to that night, I can see now that Robert and his brother were both shaking their heads, glaring at me and trying to do everything to change the subject and tell me to shut up. But Tina was curious to know what I meant when I said Tom was "capable" and I thought we were all being honest and open so I told her he was a good fuck. She asked, "Oh! And how would you know that?" And I said, "Well, because he's fucked me a few times and I thought he was pretty good."'

Cringing from that memory, Rosie says, 'It was probably about then that I realised I'd said the wrong thing. Tina walked away from me, slapped Tom across the face, and then stormed out of the house. Robert said it was his brother's fault for being adulterous, and Tom blamed Robert for not telling me to keep my big mouth shut. I blamed both of them for allowing me to go into that situation without knowing what I could and couldn't say. Luckily Tom was able to make things up with his wife by lying to her.' With a bitter snort, Rosie says, 'He explained that I have mental issues and told her I've got the lousiest sense of humour in the world. They're still married. And Tom still goes with other women behind Tina's back. But that evening put an end to Tom joining me and Robert for voyeurism and threesomes. I told Robert I wasn't comfortable having sex with a married man whose wife didn't know he was being unfaithful and he sympathised and understood. I've made a point, ever since, to only fuck lads who are either single, or who are with their wives while I'm fucking them and keeping to those simple rules has meant I've enjoyed some pretty good sex.' She smiles contentedly and says, 'Once we've started a family, I'm looking forward to getting back to the threesomes and being watched so I can have a properly satisfying sex life again.'

SECRETS

> **Can You Keep a Secret?** Middle-aged
> couple, both bi, want similar for fun and
> friendship. Open to most suggestions.
> P.O. Box AL007

As mentioned in the previous chapter, the risk of exposure is perceived as a serious and real threat within the swinging lifestyle. Consequently, the need for secrecy is of paramount importance. Few members of a swinger's family and non-swinging friends are entrusted with the details of this privileged information which is part of the reason I'm so grateful to all those who have helped to make this book possible.

Swinging parents tend to keep their lifestyle secret from their children because, as one lady from London pithily explained, 'It's hard enough telling your kids about the birds and the bees. Following that awkward conversation by saying, "Oh! And that's what Mummy and Daddy do on a weekend with Uncle Ted and Auntie Betty," would probably make their little heads spin round.'

Similarly, although there are exceptions, swinging children seldom tell their parents explicit details about their recreational activities. Because parents are usually the first choice for baby-sitters, this often necessitates invented stories, fanciful fabrications and outright lies in order to explain regular attendance at late-night parties.

Some single swingers do confide in their parents and with varying degrees of acceptance. One single bi female in Scotland explained that her mother knows all about the parties she attends – and doesn't approve. Since honestly admitting her lifestyle choice, the single bi female's mother has repeatedly nagged at her to 'see the error of her ways', and threatened that, if she doesn't stop, 'her father will find out about it'. Conversely, a single male swinger from Tyneside admitted that since he had confessed about swinging to his parents, his mother now buys clothes that she thinks would flatter him at forthcoming parties. A single female swinger in Cornwall said that her mother guessed she was going out to parties, and then explained she recognised the signs from her own days of attending swinging parties.

But single swingers seem to be the anomaly as far as the secrecy of swinging is concerned and those who are married or in established relationships usually keep their lifestyle a closely guarded secret. The most often stated reason for this was probably best summarised by a Welsh husband who said, 'Mary might have secrets that she wants to share with her friends, and I might have secrets that I tell my friends. But swinging is *our* secret and if either of us tells anyone about it, we're revealing our spouse's secret.'

Some couples maintain that the shared secret brings them closer together. Many swinging couples describe their relationship as extremely close to begin with but being involved in the shared secret of swinging invokes an intimacy that strengthens that existing bond. A lady in Yorkshire explained, 'It's like we've got something extra that no other couple has. We've got each other. We've got a tremendous sex life. And we've got the big shared secret of our swinging.'

But for others, the cognitive dissonance that comes from being honest with their partner and duplicitous with everyone else can prove irreconcilable and has driven many otherwise satisfied swingers away from the lifestyle. The couples on the following pages have been kind enough to share some of their most closely guarded secrets.

Sonia is thirty-four years old, married to Stephen, and the mother of four children. A full-time mother, Sonia divides her time between working on the volunteer committee of the PTA at her children's school during weekday evenings and swinging with Stephen on a weekend. Sonia and Stephen have been married for twelve years and swinging for three and live just outside the north-west seaside resort of Blackpool.

Sonia: 'One of the swingers' websites we visit regularly, I can't remember if it was Swinging Heaven or Swing Fans or a different one, used to have this jokey page on one of its forums. It was called "*You Know Your Neighbour's a Swinger When . . .*" and it had all these truisms that certainly rang a bell with me. There were things like, "*You Know Your Neighbour's a Swinger When they hold lots of late night parties but never invite you.*" Or "*You Know Your Neighbour's a Swinger When they spend Monday through Friday living for the weekend and, when you ask them what they do on the weekend, they just shrug and look guilty and then change the subject.*" My favourite was the one that said, "*You're baby-sitting for the neighbours as they go out to a formal dinner party and he's carrying a box of condoms and she's wearing a micro-mini and a peephole bra.*" That sounded just like us.'

Sonia and Stephen are sitting in a Blackpool swingers' club for our interview. It's not customary for swingers' clubs to allow single male reporters into their establishments. I've been granted a special dispensation by the owner who read and enjoyed *Swingers: True Confessions From Today's Swinging Scene*. A framed (and signed) copy of the book's cover takes pride of place on the wall behind the bar. Although Sonia isn't wearing a micro-mini and a peephole bra, it has to be conceded that her outfit is very revealing. The couple have plans to enjoy the facilities of the swingers' club after our interview and Sonia constantly scans the door as newcomers enter.

'So many of those jokes made me think that was how we were living our lives,' Sonia continues. 'If the page had been seen by someone who knew us, especially someone like my mother-in-law, I was worried they might put two and two together. Stephen's mother baby-sits for us whenever we go to the club. We couldn't come here if not for her. When you're picking a baby-sitter for whilst you're going to a party it has to be someone you can trust completely and someone who doesn't mind being there until the early hours of the morning – or later if things pan out that way. Swinging isn't something where you can say, "Yes, we'll be home by midnight," and always be home by midnight because sometimes things don't start to develop until around that time of night or later, and the best things can happen when plans suddenly change.'

Sonia looks at her husband and he nods agreement.

'A couple of months ago we went to a party that started at eight on an evening,' Sonia continues. 'It was an hour's drive away so that meant we had to leave Stephen's mother baby-sitting at seven. We'd planned to leave at midnight and be home for about one and she said she was OK with us coming back at that time. It was a good party. We chatted with a few people and played with some others and managed to spend a couple of hours in the playroom when it got really busy. As we were leaving Stephen ended up chatting with this couple who'd rented a room in a nearby motel. They asked if we fancied joining them for an hour or so alone and, after Stephen had phoned his mother and told her we'd be home later than expected, we went back to the motel with them.'

Stephen interrupts to tell us it was a good night and Sonia agrees wholeheartedly. 'It was a good night. They were looking for a full swap, we were both fired up for that, and we had a great time together creating our own little mini-orgy. We're both bi, and they were both bi, so we got the chance to pair off twice before joining together as a foursome. Ordinarily that would have been as much as we could manage for one evening but, as we were leaving their room, we bumped into another couple from the party who were also booked in at the same motel. They recognised us . . .'

Stephen explains that the four of them had come close to shagging in the playroom at the party.

'. . . and they invited us to join them in their room,' Sonia concludes. 'Stephen phoned his mother again and we had another private swap with that couple. They weren't bisexual. Or at least, he wasn't bisexual. But she was up for anything and we really had an awful lot of fun with them. We eventually got back home at about seven in the morning, telling Stephen's mother that we'd ended up chatting with friends, lost track of the time, and hadn't wanted to risk the long drive home with Stephen being too tired to be safe behind the wheel.'

With obvious gratitude, Sonia says, 'No other baby-sitter could have been so accepting of the situation. Only Stephen's mother would be able to put up with spending twelve hours looking after our kids and then receiving such a weak explanation for where we'd been and what we'd been doing. I don't know if Stephen's mother fully believes what we tell her. We both know she wouldn't accept or understand what we do at the parties, so we just don't tell her. I don't like to think of it as lying – it's more like I'm not upsetting her with a truth she wouldn't want to hear.' She smiles without humour and nods. 'I know how shallow that sounds but I honestly don't think she could handle learning that her precious Stephen goes out for lots of naughty adult sex romps and has probably sucked more cock than his wife. But I don't like lying or concealing the truth from her and it's never easy.'

A couple enter the club and Sonia waves to them. She ushers Stephen to go and join them and tells him she'll only be another five minutes concluding the interview. Returning briskly to the subject she says, 'Because we usually visit a club I like to dress appropriately. I've got the legs for a short skirt and I like to wear low-cut tops that leave little to the imagination.'

Sonia stands up and shows off her legs which are remarkably attractive in sheer black stockings. 'The first time Stephen's mother saw me dressed for a party she almost died. She was saying, "What the bloody hell are you wearing? You can't go out like that. You're practically naked. You look like a whore." It was a complete overreaction and I could have killed all her arguments by simply saying I was going to a swingers' party and I wanted to look totally shaggable.' Sonia smiles and grimly adds, 'But I couldn't ever say that to her. Instead, I told her I was only wearing what all the other women at the club would be wearing, which wasn't really a lie.'

She gestures to the few women who have already appeared at the club and it's obvious that Sonia's revealing ensemble is not much more daring than anything else being worn in the club. 'I think I was wearing spiked heels, fishnets, a leather mini and a leather corset the first time she saw me going out to a party. I'd got a coat over the outfit, so I was decent for while we were driving down here, but you could see the veins bulging on my mother-in-law's forehead as though she was about to have some sort of episode. To appease her I tried dressing down for a while in longer skirts or less-revealing blouses, but that just meant the parties were less fun for me because I looked drab compared to some of the more glamorous women that were there. To compensate, I once dressed in jeans and a jumper and then stripped naked while I was in the car. It made for a good entrance, taking my coat off and being starkers in the middle of this place, but it was more ostentatious than I like to be and I only did that a couple of times before deciding that the short skirts and revealing tops were more erotic than total nudity.'

Sonia considers her legs again and says thoughtfully, 'Also, I prefer to wear stockings when I go to the club. I know that men go crazy for the sight of a woman in stockings and I know it affects a lot of women in the same way too. The majority of women that I've been with have been wearing stockings and they've all looked sexy because of them. I also like the feel of hold-ups squeezing at the tops of my thighs and it's one of the sexiest things to have a stranger's fingers stroking the bare flesh above the top of my stockings.'

Glancing over at Stephen and nodding, she seems to remember that our interview is due to end soon and hurries to make her point. 'Eventually I ended up going back to wearing the clothes I wanted to wear for the club. Fishnet, minis and corsets, mainly. I still do it, even though Stephen's mother clearly disapproves. Over the years she's grown more tolerant of me "dressing like a whore", as she calls it, but I still wonder if she totally buys into the lies that I feed her.'

Sonia's mood is suddenly reflective. Although Stephen and the other couple are gesturing for her to join them she waves dismissively in their direction. 'I think that's the thing that worries me the most. If Stephen's mum ever found out we were swinging I know she would refuse to baby-sit for us, and that would effectively kill our swinging. There's no one I'd trust more in looking after the kids and I couldn't enjoy myself at a party if I didn't think the kids were safe with a responsible adult. I'd be happier if I could tell her we were going to a party but I feel sure she'd disown us. I don't like keeping the truth from her but the only other option is to tell her and meet with her incvitable disapproval and I can't see we're ever going to do that. I suppose, as long as me and Stephen are able to keep our secret, we can all be happy. We can still carry on swinging and Stephen's mother can carry on baby-sitting for us. But if our secret ever comes out, I think there will be some pretty big changes in our lives and I don't think all of them will be for the better.'

Tiffany works as a legal secretary in Cardiff. The mother of two daughters, she has been married to Tony for sixteen years and the couple have been swinging for five. Tiffany describes herself as bisexual but 'dependent on circumstances'. When asked to explain Tiffany says she prefers sex with women when she and Tony go to clubs or parties, and she favours the company of men when they are meeting another couple for a private foursome.

Tiffany: 'The secrecy is what makes swinging so exciting for me. Tony acts like he's James Bond with the whole espionage thing and I can understand that. It's almost as though we're living two separate lives: respectable family members by day, hardcore swingers by night. Going from one of those worlds to the other is a fantastic thrill.'

Tony has not been able to join us for the interview but Tiffany talks about him so often it's almost as though he is an unseen presence in the room. 'Whenever we can, we meet up for lunch from the office. Last Wednesday Tony met me at our usual café and we got to talking about a forthcoming party. It was only a small thing: I'd spent the morning doing the school run, then working in my job as secretary for a local firm of solicitors. Then I was having a civilised lunch with my husband and we were chatting about a potential orgy; the number of guys I was hoping to screw; the sorts of women he wanted to shag; and reminiscing about previous parties and what we'd done. I was bubbling by the time I got back to the office but I had to sit there through the last four hours of the day, acting as though I was all innocent and pretending I wasn't ready to jump anyone who walked into the office. We had a great session when I got back home that evening and the arousal allowed me to focus on what we'd be doing when we visited the club at the weekend.' When it's mentioned that she and Tony clearly share a strong bond, Tiffany nods proudly. 'Sharing the secret with Tony keeps the excitement constant. Throughout the working day he'll send me text messages, asking me if I'm looking for cock or pussy at the next party. Answering those questions when other people are around, being so bold as to write I WANT COCK while my boss is chatting on the phone beside me, or the office's other secretary is talking to me about the latest celebrity gossip, reinforces the fact that Tony and I have a huge secret that no one would ever guess. And our world is always like that.'

After showing photographs of Tony, Tiffany has put on the TV to show a video of her and her husband with another couple. The tape plays in the background as we talk and Tiffany repeatedly glances at the screen whenever the camera focuses on her husband.

'Our regular weekday routine is for us both to get up between six and seven. I'll get the kids ready for school while Tony does breakfast. He sets off for work at eight and I take the kids out ten minutes later, dropping them off early for school so I'm not too late getting into my office. I'm known for being quiet and efficient in the office – the exact opposite to what I'm like when we hit a club. I might see Tony for lunch some days but most days we can't manage to meet up throughout the day. At the end of the day we'll play with the girls until bedtime and then we'll either go to bed and play with each other, or we'll surf the net looking for potential partners.' The routine sounds comparable to the schedule of many other swinging couples interviewed for this book.

'The only time it's been any different,' Tiffany begins carefully, 'was when one of the temps my boss employed turned out to be an occasional visitor from our local swingers' club. I'd recognised her instantly – she was a bisexual submissive and pretty enough to be memorable. When I saw her in the office, looking as lost as most temps do, I didn't know what to do at first. I was very nervous that she was going to recognise me and say something embarrassing but, as it turned out, she didn't remember me at all. I wasn't upset by that.' She gestures towards the video as though this explains her last remark.

'The swinging Tiffany and the non-swinging Tiffany are two totally different people. Tony has said that I seem taller and more powerful when we're out at a party. In the office I just hunch my shoulders, get my head down, and try to get my work done so it's over with and not interfering with my private life. I think I come across as quiet and shy and withdrawn in the office. I also think, because I wear glasses in the office and contacts when we're partying, it must look like a contrast between Superman and Clark Kent.'

Her comments do make sense. Looking at the vivacious woman in the video, holding an erection in each hand and smiling saucily for the camera, it's hard to accept she's the same woman as the bespectacled secretary holding the remote.

'Before I spoke to the temp, I texted Tony and told him that Wendy was working in my office. He texted back to ask if I was going to try and shag her in my lunch break. The idea of doing it got me very horny. But I knew I was never going to act on it. Nevertheless, I took every opportunity I could to work close with Wendy. I took her under my wing, showed her how to process the various files we dealt with and even took her out to lunch a couple of times so that she didn't feel so isolated. That was when I decided to let her know who I was.' Tiffany puts a hand over her mouth to contain a grin. It's only in that moment, when she's smiling wickedly, that she looks anything like the woman on the TV screen.

'Because we were the only ones working in the office – she was covering for a fortnight while the other secretary was away on annual leave – I figured there was little chance of her gossiping my secret to anyone. The bosses are a bunch of snobs and don't socialise with secretaries, let alone temps, so there was no danger of her saying anything to them. She didn't know anyone else from the firm so I felt safe in confiding to her. And I had the feeling Wendy was going to eventually work out where she'd seen me because she kept telling me my face looked vaguely familiar and she was sure she knew me from somewhere outside the office. We were alone in the café when she said that again. I shrugged and said, "Perhaps you glanced at my face a few months back while you were eating my pussy?"

'You've never seen anyone go so red.

'She looked so shocked I was almost ashamed with myself. I explained that I recognised her from a party and she was absolutely astonished that I was the same Tiffany that she'd finger-fucked and licked two months earlier. She kept telling me that I just didn't look like someone who would go to a party and I promised her, the next time we met up at a party, she'd see I was one and the same person. Not that it took us that long to get together.

'Once Wendy realised that we both had the same inclinations she turned into the most terrible tease. She'd sit closer to me in the office and reveal the tops of her stockings, or let me see that her blouse was very open and showing off an indecent amount of cleavage. Each time I took her through a new procedure on the accounts system she would grasp it quickly enough but, whenever she made a mistake, she'd suggest that she needed punishing.

'It was very hard to concentrate on the work.

'I was very turned on by the idea of shagging Wendy. Because she was extremely submissive I knew I could do anything I wanted with her. And I also knew, I would only have to give instructions, and she would obey me completely. I texted Tony to tell him that working so close to Wendy was getting me really horny and he said I should just go ahead and shag her.' Tiffany grins at Tony's image on the TV screen. He's standing behind a blonde and riding her vigorously from behind.

'I told my bosses that I needed to work late that night to catch up with some stuff that had back-logged while I brought the temp up to speed with our processes. They bought that, and also accepted that I'd need to have the temp with me, to help me get the workload reduced. Then I told Wendy she was working late, that we were going to be alone in the office and I was going to be in charge.'

Tiffany laughs and explains the behaviour fell outside her usual parameters of what was safe or acceptable. But the opportunity to play alone with Wendy was too tempting.

'I could see she was as excited and anxious as I was. I'm not usually into being dominant during sex. I know what I want and I feel comfortable telling a partner about my needs and offering suggestions for how they can be best met. But I don't think I'm really a dominant person. Not sexually. But I didn't have any problems telling Wendy that I wanted her kneeling on the floor in front of me. I got her to lick my pussy and finger me and then I licked her while she was bent across my desk.'

Muting the video, because the cries in the background have become a little louder than either of us can tolerate, Tiffany says again, 'The strangest thing about that first time in the office with Wendy was that I was bringing my sex life dangerously close to my office life. I usually keep the two as very separate, compartmentalised items. Finding Wendy working as a temp in the office was something of a shock that brought those two worlds very close together. But actually taking the decision to shag her there brought them crashing into one another. Of course, I couldn't take Wendy home because we have the girls here. Also, Tony would have wanted to join in if we'd been here and, as selfish as it sounds, I wanted Wendy for myself. I couldn't have waited until Wendy next showed up at a party because that could have taken ages to happen and the saucy mare had made me desperate to have her again as soon as possible. With Wendy having worked through about half of her fortnight's contract at the office, I figured it made sense to let my swinging life overlap with my office life for once.' With a self-satisfied smile she says, 'And I managed it very well. I got Wendy to do three or four nights of overtime in her final week and we did some pretty outrageous things together. I'd never tried fisting before but Wendy seemed to live for it. She wanted us to do watersports but, although I tried it with her in the office loos, it wasn't such a great turn-on for me. Perhaps it was because I don't find toilets to be a sexy place. There was a bit of a thrill watching her wee and hearing her beg for me to wee on her. So perhaps it was just environment that was a turn-off for that particular thing. But other than the watersports, Wendy seemed to know what would turn me on and we screwed each other regularly through those last few days while she worked at the office. I used my mobile to send pictures through to Tony and he got very excited by them – excited enough to screw me two or three times each night when I got back home.'

Glancing again at her husband on the video, Tiffany says, 'Wendy agreed to meet us at our local club for the weekend after she'd finished working in the office. That gave Tony another chance to screw her. They played for a little while but there was no real chemistry between them. He admitted afterwards that he had never been particularly drawn to her, even when he'd seen her at the club the first time. But he did enjoy screwing me at the club while Wendy was licking my pussy and his balls.' She tears her gaze away from the onscreen version of Tony and mumbles a comment about them having different tastes in some things. 'That's the only time I've ever let my swinging life come close to my working life,' she adds. 'I don't think I'd do it again because I was very worried that I'd be found out. It was a lot of fun doing Wendy in the office. It was worth the late nights. But it was also quite draining. One of the bosses said I looked really tired after doing so much overtime and I got really panicked that he'd found out what I'd been doing and was making a subtle reference to my screwing Wendy across his desk. I'm certain that wasn't what he meant. He's never made any reference to it since and I've got no reason to suspect that my secret is known to anyone at the office. But it was enough to make me cautious and I no longer do anything in the office that could result in me being exposed as a swinger. However, I do still see Wendy from time to time at our local club and I always make a point of spending some time with her when we're in the same place together.'

Uma is thirty and has been married for six years and swinging for three. Living near Maidstone, Uma works on the factory floor of a food-processing plant. In her contact ads she describes herself as having a full and curvy figure and tries to leave her DD cup bra size (the girls, as she calls them) as a pleasant surprise for those couples she meets face-to-face.

Uma: 'I found it very hard to keep the secret of our swinging at first. It's such a big secret that you feel like you're going to burst if you don't tell someone. Like all swinging couples, we were able to confide in each other, and in some ways that did make it seem more special. It brought us closer. But there were other times, when I was at work or with friends or family, when a part of me longed to blurt it all out and tell everyone what I'd been doing and boast about how special swinging had made my life.'

Uma smokes while she talks. We are sitting outside her home in a back garden that has been painstakingly recreated to look like a tranquil Japanese rockery. Uma maintains that the garden is her husband's handiwork but she seems genuinely relaxed in this suburban oasis.

'We started swinging about three years into our marriage. The sex before that was good, very enjoyable, but we wanted to see if we could make it better. I'd got lots of fantasies about going with women, going with other men, or maybe doing group stuff like an orgy or something. My husband has always been supportive and he wanted me to fulfil all of my fantasies. Because he had no problems about me going with anyone else, I accepted the level of openness in our marriage as something really special. I didn't mind him going with other women. Being honest, the idea was quite a turn-on for me and, since we've been swinging, I've found that watching that happen has always been enough of a stimulus to help me orgasm.'

Uma has no need to explain this any further. We were introduced at a swingers' club earlier in the year. At that venue Uma's voyeuristic appreciation of her husband with two women was made apparent. When this party is mentioned Uma nods and agrees that the evening was a memorable night. 'We had it good for our first year,' she explains. 'We eased into swinging through contact ads online at first and then through parties. Our first ever swing was with a couple the same age as us and we were all newbies. I've spoken to other couples since and a lot of them claim they were lucky because they were introduced to swinging by a more experienced couple. But, because all four of us were completely inexperienced, we were able to educate ourselves. The four of us had each had a drink, we were at theirs, and the conversation eventually turned to sex. We all admitted that we had no idea how to go about a swap and all four of us had different notions about how it should happen. The other couple thought it should be done in separate rooms. We thought it should be done in the same room. The guys wanted to see the girls copping off and both us girls wanted to be fucked by two guys simultaneously.' She finishes her cigarette and carefully stubs it into an ashtray, so as not to spoil the uncluttered splendour of the rockery.

'It was frustrating but fun,' Uma remembers. 'A little like staring at a Rubik's cube and knowing how it should look when it's solved but not having the faintest idea of how to get it there. I came up with the idea of us each, one after the other, tossing a coin. If it landed heads you got to ask someone else in the room to do something for you. If it landed tails you had to get someone to do something for your partner. It was a simple game but very effective and it really worked to get us all at ease with each other. Things started off slowly, with just kisses and undressing. Nothing unexpected and nothing overtly outrageous. But enough to get us all very excited and aroused. Things started to heat up when my husband threw a tails and said he wanted the other girl in the room to suck one of my nipples.

'I almost came when she was easing my boob out of the cup of my bra. When she started to suck against me I was in absolute heaven. My hands were shaking so badly I couldn't toss the coin properly afterwards and everyone was laughing at me. But not in an unkind way. And, as a first time, I think it was better that we didn't meet up with an experienced couple because we learnt from each other and ourselves and I think that sort of independence has always been important to me. I think the only problem with learning the way we did was that there was no one there to reinforce the message on us that we needed to keep the details of our swinging secret from other people.'

Frowning, Uma lights another cigarette.

'On that first evening we got to do about half of the things we'd wanted. I got to kiss and touch a woman. I got kissed and touched by a woman. It was nothing outrageous. She sucked my nips and I fingered her pussy. Then I sucked another man while my husband watched and he fucked another woman while I watched.' Giggling as she snorts smoke through her nostrils, Uma says, 'I have never come so hard in my entire life. It's not an understatement to say it changed our lives. It certainly changed my life. From that point on I was just living for the swinging. Just living for the sex. I can't explain why it was better. When I've thought back on it I keep stumbling on the whole secrecy thing and maybe that was what did it for me. We'd meet another couple. The four of us would go behind a closed door. And then we'd do things that were meant to remain behind that door. We'd do things that adults don't usually do unless they're married or living together or at least very very drunk.

'The size of the girls made me very popular at parties.' Uma grins, glancing down at her ample bosom. 'In that first year, I got to go all the way with a woman. That was a very intense experience. I watched my husband go with a dozen different women and he must have seen me with as many different men. If not more. A couple of times, well a few if I'm being honest, I had my husband in my backside while another man was fucking me the regular way. I climaxed repeatedly. Sometimes I climaxed so hard it physically hurt. I loved every second of it. Which is why I should have kept it a secret.'

There's a long moment's silence while we both concentrate on smoking in the tranquillity of the rockery. 'I made the mistake of telling my sister,' Uma says eventually. 'I don't like to think that I was bragging but that was probably part of it. Until you've been swinging, and until you've experienced the thrill of getting so much pleasure that the rest of the world seems to be overlooking, you don't realise what a big thing it is to have to keep to yourself.

'My sister was round at ours one evening, complaining about her boyfriend, and saying that she thought he was screwing around behind her back. I made the usual sympathetic sounds that sisters are supposed to make but the truth was I couldn't see it as that big a problem. If she wasn't happy with it, I thought she should dump him. If she loved him, I figured she should embrace it and live the lifestyle. I thought about saying that but even I wasn't thick enough to believe that was the proper way for one sister to console another. Then she asked, "What would you do?" '

Sighing, Uma says, 'I tried to tell her that it wasn't my problem, and we were talking about her boyfriend and not my husband. But she insisted on an answer and kept pressing saying, "What would you do? What would you do if you thought your man was screwing around behind your back?" I said, "Being honest, if I thought he was having fun it wouldn't trouble me." I went on to try and tell her that it was the "behind my back" part that would upset me more than him going with another woman but she wanted to know what the hell I meant.'

Uma's cigarette is down to the filter but she doesn't appear to have noticed. It sits forgotten between her fingertips. 'My sister said, "Are you telling me that you wouldn't mind if your husband screwed another woman?" And I said it wouldn't trouble me in the slightest. She said she didn't believe me and I said, "Well, I've watched him screw a dozen women so far this year and it's not been a problem. What more proof do you need?" Open mouth. Insert foot.'

Carefully, Uma stubs her cigarette into the ashtray.

'I can see now that my sister just wasn't in the mood to accept what I was saying. At first she thought I was saying that my husband got to go with other women and made me watch. She called me a doormat. Patiently I explained that she had misunderstood. I explained about the swinging. I told her we saw other couples. I said that sometimes I'd have sex with women. Sometimes I'd have sex with men. Sometimes I'd have sex with everyone who was in the room. And I tried to tell her that jealousy was never an issue because I wasn't jealous of my husband and he wasn't jealous of me. I tried to tell her that we were there for each other and were using the swinging to explore our sexual boundaries but she wasn't listening.'

Uma glances at her pack of cigarettes but refrains from taking one out. 'She called me a slut – a depraved slut – and said she couldn't talk to me any more. Which was pretty hurtful and upsetting. My husband was sympathetic but he spent a lot of time telling me that I shouldn't have mentioned anything to my sister. And I didn't really need to hear the words "I told you so" so many times. But I could understand his anger because I had come close to spoiling the swinging. My sister's not known for keeping secrets. Most people, even her boyfriend, refer to her as a mouthy bitch, so it's easy to see why my husband thought she was exactly the wrong person to tell. But I'd been in an awkward situation. I was being asked for advice about matters of sex and fidelity; I felt as though I had a relevant insight into the topic; and I made a misjudgement.' With a bitter laugh she says, 'That one stupid slip had some long-reaching effects. Most importantly it took some of the pleasure away from the sex. I don't know how to say that better. Before I spoke to my sister the sex had always been good. Whether we'd been with another couple or just together; either talking about what we'd done with other couples or planning what we'd do with the next pair: I kept thinking that I was the one who had put our swinging lifestyle in danger. I was the one who had given away the secret. My husband didn't mention it any more after the night it happened. But I always felt that his anger at my stupidity was lurking between us.'

Although Uma's house is close to a main road, with loud buses and cars passing by at regular intervals, the rockery is surprisingly tranquil. When we're both sat in silence it's like being at the end of the earth.

'The sex was tainted too,' Uma admits after a pause. 'I'm not trying to say I was sexually dysfunctional or anything. My libido was still running on overdrive and I was usually up for most anything. But it would get to a certain point in the evening and I would realise I was trying something different and I'd think of my sister calling me a depraved slut and it would sour the mood a little. That happened once when I was licking my husband's semen from deep inside a woman's pussy. I suddenly got an image of my sister in my mind and she was calling me a depraved slut and I wondered: Is she right?'

Uma finally gives in and takes another cigarette from her pack. She lights it before continuing. 'It also happened when I was trying to squeeze two cocks into my pussy. The situation should have been really arousing. I'd screwed both guys, the woman of the couple had had enough, and my husband and this other man were both hard and I wanted them. They were trying to work it so that, as one cock slid out, the other slipped inside me. I was pressed between two sexy guys. I was definitely in the mood for trying it. But I just remembered that my sister thought I was a depraved slut and, even though I told myself I didn't care what she thought, I wondered if she was right. It didn't help that I knew if I discussed it with anyone, anyone who wasn't into swinging, they'd tell me I was a depraved slut for getting double-banged or drinking spent come from a woman's pussy.

'And I knew my sister had told other people. She didn't say she had told people. And no one ever said anything to my face. But I could see from the way people were looking at me that they were seeing me in a different light. Some guys would smirk when I went into the room and nudge each other. Women would glare at me and then grab their husbands, as though they were scared I was going to jump them then and there. But it did help teach me about keeping things quiet.'

Uma blows a long plume of smoke into the air and grins tightly. 'When a group of girls were sat round in the canteen recently, all of them chatting about Jude Law and what they would do to him, I ignored the conversation. Even when one of them threw her copy of *Hello!* at me and asked me if I'd screw him, I just shook my head and reminded her I was a married woman.' She brightens a little when she says, 'My sister has now started speaking to me again. It took a year. She started talking with me again at around the same time as she kicked her boyfriend into touch. But I'm not trying to suggest those two facts are related. Neither of us have mentioned the reason why we stopped speaking for a year. I don't think we ever will. But that doesn't really trouble me. Since we've started talking again I've no longer felt like a depraved slut while I've been with another couple.' Winking sombrely, Uma says, 'Well, I haven't felt like a depraved slut in the bad way. And I have learnt my lesson about keeping secrets.'

EXTREMES

Sex is measured in extremes. Couples go *all the way*. Sexual
encounters are recalled as being *out-of-this-world*. Contact
ads often refer to full penetrative intercourse as *the ultimate*
(i.e. couple seek couple for same-room fun, including the
ultimate). This vocabulary of extremes is already straining
with superlatives as it describes attractiveness, satisfaction
and simple sexual intercourse, but that doesn't stop swinging singles and couples from stretching boundaries, pushing
the envelope and trying to boldly go where no one has gone
before.

It's difficult to ascribe this need for excess to anything
other than greed. We live in a capitalist society where
consumption is encouraged and success is measured in
achievement of extremes. Away from sex we aspire to own
cars that are the fastest and most desirable. We are urged to
wear clothes and jewellery rated as the most stylish,
expensive or prestigious. We rush to possess gadgets that

are promoted as being the latest advance in state-of-the-art technology. As an extension of this acquisitive nature, when it comes to sexual experiences, many unconsciously subscribe to the *Wall Street* credo: 'Greed is good.'

This attitude is most obviously epitomised in the phenomenon of greedy girls' nights. These parties are organised with a small number of females (usually two or three) balanced against a greater number of males (as many as a dozen and upwards). The premise behind these parties is that the 'greedy girls' can enjoy a large number of consecutive male partners within the same sexual experience. But, while these parties might epitomise the swinging equivalent of our society's desire to constantly consume and attain new extremes, they are not the only example. Marathon events are organised for both sexes, the quality of partners is often measured in the quantitive extremes of largest or longest, and many swingers rate the superiority of playrooms on their capacity or the vast numbers in attendance.

Not that every swinger takes their recreation to extremes. There are many male swingers who can seldom manage to satisfy more than one female partner in an evening. The majority of soft-swingers are content in only being with their established partner and enjoying the ambience of the soft-swing environment as a peripheral pleasure. A lot of the couples interviewed for this book and its predecessor wouldn't entertain the idea of seeing more than another couple in one evening. And, although orgies, group sex and greedy girl events are sensationally popularised, a vast number of female swingers are satisfied with having simply one or two penetrative experiences in a swinging evening.

But this chapter is about extremes. The incidents reported on the following pages don't represent the majority of swingers and their experiences. Conversely, these are just a small proportion of women with an appetite for excess who have realised the opportunity to achieve their ambitions. Their contributions are included here to show that, even though many swingers tend to conservatism in their life-style, and refute the stories of mammoth orgies, greedy girls and gratuitous excess, these extremes are regularly achieved within the swinging community.

Valerie is thrity-one years old and single. She is medium height with a slender, athletic figure. She has been a swinger since her late teens and has been a regular patron of several swingers' clubs in and around Newcastle.

Valerie: 'Yes. I've done some extreme things. I suppose most people would be shocked by half of the things I've done. I can even shock swingers and hardcore fetishists, so I must have done some extreme things. But I think that's me. I like to shock people. I like to go further than anyone else would dare. I like to shock myself.'

Her statement is not easy to process. Valerie is a slender woman, looks younger than her thirty-one years and, on the surface, seems incapable of shocking. She wears a pair of black Lycra leggings and a multi-coloured tunic, the uni-form of a hundred young women who have passed us while we chat in the shopping centre's coffee shop. The only thing about her appearance that suggests she might be able to shock are the BCR [Ball Closure Ring] piercings in her nose, lip and ears.

'I lost my virginity early,' Valerie explains. 'At a party. I'd given hand jobs and blowies before but I'd never gone all the way with a boy. At the party where I lost my cherry one of these lads said he wanted to fuck me and I just said, "OK." His friend watched us, and then he fucked me too. Before I knew what was happening a queue had formed and

I had half a dozen lads that night. That must have been a sign of things to come.'

When she laughs, Valerie reveals the piercing in her tongue.

'My first steady boyfriend, the first one I was serious about, he got me into swinging. I was young and pretty, which meant I was fairly popular whenever we went to a club or a house party. I could guarantee getting as many cocks as I wanted. I could also guarantee getting any woman in the place too. I'd just have to bat my eyelids and give them my I-wanna-fuck-you look and they'd be all over me. Men and women. And, for a while, I was fairly content with that.'

When Valerie brushes the hair from her face she reveals that her ears have been pierced many times. A row of a dozen or more studs decorates the helix and lobe.

'That was probably why I got a reputation for being something of a goer. A few of the clubs I visited kept calling me, telling me they needed me at the club to liven up a dull night, or asking me if I could come the next night or the next week because they were expecting it to be busy and they knew I'd liven things up. And, if I wasn't doing anything, I'd happily go. It's nice to be popular and, if the rewards of being popular include free party invites, free drinks and lots of sex then I usually got fairly well rewarded.'

The coffee shop is fairly busy but Valerie doesn't lower her voice. And, although Valerie is admitting to promiscuity and hedonism, her revelations still don't seem particularly shocking.

'I tried group and I did that regularly for a long time. I liked group a lot because it's almost like bondage, but with human bodies instead of ropes, cuffs or straps. When you're in a playroom, and pinned down by a load of naked people, and you can't move for bare arms and legs and pussies and cocks, it really is exciting. One of the good things I liked about group was that I never knew who was doing what to me. The mystery of thinking, "Those fingers inside me feel really good, I wonder who they belong to?" always got me very excited. Trying to decide if I was being tongued by a man or a woman would usually get me coming. I liked being able to turn my face one way to kiss a girl or a guy, and then turn in the other direction to find I could suck a cock or lick a pussy or rim an ass. It was an extreme experience and for a long time it was the only reason I went to clubs.'

The lady at a nearby table has overheard Valerie's statement and fixes her with a contemptuous glare. Valerie is either oblivious to the lady or simply ignoring her.

'Then I got a little tired of doing the group thing. I don't know why I got tired of it. I think, because I'd spent about six months doing nothing but group I was just a bit too used to it. Bored – for want of a better word. I still found it exciting to be writhing around with dozens of naked bodies, but I think I was so familiar with it that I needed something different.'

The lady at the nearby table vacates her seat with a loud snort of disgust. Valerie glances at her and grins. 'I tried doing men only for a while. That was fun, and very different from the group experience. That was when I tried my first greedy girls' night, probably before they were called greedy girls' nights. There was one party where I had thirty blokes in the same night. Everyone was saying it must have been some sort of record and I've never heard any woman admit she's had so many men in the same night. Of course, it's not something that many women would admit to but even in the most serious swinging circles I know a lot of people think that figure's high enough to be nearly unbelievable but it must have been somewhere around there. I stopped counting after twenty.' She laughs and says, 'I've got to admit, my pussy was red raw by the end of that night. I got home and had spunk in my hair and all over my body. My tits were caked in the stuff, I even found some in my armpit, and I ached from all the exertion. But I did enjoy it because I was doing my men-only thing. It was during that period that I'd hang around with two or three guys at a club and just spend the entire night either playing with their cocks, sitting on their cocks or trying to take two or three men at the same time.' She reflects on this for a moment before adding, 'It was satisfying in lots and lots of different ways. I enjoy being penetrated and there are so many different sensations you get from cock that it always seemed like I was experiencing something new. Some guys are thicker than others. Some guys are longer or shaped differently with a bend to the left or a kink to the right. You get different tastes from some guys and they all have different ways of using their cocks. I really did enjoy becoming a cock-connoisseur but, eventually, I got bored. Someone started telling me I have a low attention span but I didn't listen to all of what they were saying. That's a joke. But it probably contains a grain of truth. I don't think I get bored easily. I just think, when it comes to sex, I get obsessed about something, get totally fixated on it, and then it's all-or-nothing on that one particular fetish before I decide I've done everything I can with it and I want to move on and try something else.'

Glancing around the coffee shop, Valerie frowns at the NO SMOKING sign. When it's suggested we could go outside for a cigarette she grabs her bag and we walk out of the shopping centre together. Getting back to the subject of her swinging she says, 'After my time of only going with men I then changed and tried doing women only for a while. That was nearly as satisfying, although the self-imposed restriction did make it frustrating at some points. The majority of swingers at clubs are either men or couples and the couples are usually looking for a bisexual female. I didn't mind being the female for the woman's benefit but a lot of the time the men wanted to play with me too and I'd decided that men were off limits while I was going through my women-only phase. I could see a lot of the guys were disappointed that they weren't going to get to play with me but the frustration went both ways. On more than one occasion I got very aroused by the woman I was with, but she wasn't able to completely satisfy me and I was left staring hungrily at her husband's cock and wishing I hadn't imposed such a silly limitation on what I was and wasn't allowed to do. So I think my women-only phase barely lasted three months. One night I was licking this cute blonde, well, we'd been going down on each other, and her husband was watching and stroking off and I couldn't bare the frustration any longer. I told him to fuck me and it was the hardest I'd come in ages.'

Valerie pauses, grins and admits, 'After that night, I went back to doing men and women. One of the club owners said I should try doing TVs for a while. Since I'd been on a men-only stint and then women-only, he thought I should only do guys dressed up as women. I knew he was joking with me but, if there had been more TVs at the clubs, I think I might have seriously considered the suggestion. As it was, I carried on doing men and women, making sure I enjoyed myself as fully as I could, and all the time trying not to accept that I'd grown a bit tired of swinging. I wanted something shocking and the clubs simply weren't giving it to me.' She strokes her ear between her index finger and thumb and says, 'It was probably around that time that I got my first piercing. I got my clit pierced with a small ring. I got my nipples done the following week. Two days after that I got six piercings in my inner labia – three on either side.'

The conversation moves on to the subject of piercings and their variant healing times. Limited sexual activity is advised while a genital piercing is healing. Clitoral and labial piercings can take between four to ten weeks to heal and nipple piercings can take between three and six months. Valerie concedes she was advised to limit her sexual activity but she also points out that the pack of cigarettes we are sharing advises us not to smoke.

'They hurt like hell but the look of them was sensational and it turned me on to think I'd been bold enough to get so much body jewellery. Karen, the girl who did my piercings, asked if I was into pain and BDSM. I said I'd never really tried those things and she seemed amazed. She invited me to a local dungeon and that opened up a whole new world for me.' Valerie's eyes sparkle with excitement as she admits, 'I have to say now: there's nothing better than having your arse thrashed by stinging nettles. No. I tell a lie. There is something better. There's having your arse thrashed by stinging nettles while a room full of people are watching.

'Karen took me to this fetish nightclub that was done out like a dungeon. She looked very sexy dressed up in skimpy PVC. She's very slim and sexy anyway, and it's a pleasure to be seen with her because people know that you have to be hot to be in the company of someone so sexy. But when she's wearing her PVC gear she looks outrageously attractive. And it seemed like Karen was pretty well known at the fetish club because everyone was saying hi to her, offering her drinks and generally seeming pleased to see her. She hadn't told me much about the club before we got there and, because I do like surprises, I hadn't gone out of my way to ask much. I'd simply picked up on the fact that PVC or leather was expected, black was the only colour I could confidently wear, and the experience was likely to be very different from what I'd encountered in the various swingers' clubs I'd been to.

'It started to get different when Karen led me to one wall near the bar and slipped my hands into some cuffs there. It was all very kinky. With my hands cuffed above my head I couldn't stop her – or anyone – from touching me however they wanted. I braced myself for everyone to fall on me but it was much more controlled than that.'

Outside the shopping centre, and having finished our cigarettes, Valerie suggests we talk while we walk to Karen's nearby salon.

'Karen started by just giving me a long lingering kiss. It was a tongue-wrestling kiss and got me wet but she made me stretch into it. As I was getting more and more aroused she pulled herself further and further back until the cuffs were stopping me from keeping contact with her mouth. Then she stepped back a couple of paces and watched me writhing against the wall. Then she unbuttoned my waist-coat and took my skirt off. It wasn't the first time I'd been naked in a public place. In some of the swingers' clubs I think there were some customers who'd never seen me with my clothes on. But I was comfortable in those places and familiar with everything that happened. This was a whole new experience for me and I didn't know what to expect. But Karen didn't give me a chance to say anything about that stuff. She was clearly very pleased that she'd got me naked and bound near the bar and she stood back to admire her handiwork. When I started to say I wasn't sure about the situation she told me that she'd gag me if I said another word. That really excited me.'

Reaching the tattoo parlour and body-piercing salon where Karen works, our conversation is interrupted as Valerie makes introductions. Karen is busy with a client, tattooing an ornate Celtic design on to the lower back of a young woman. Our conversation continues as Karen finishes the artwork. 'I think that first night with Karen was probably part of what helped me decide the fetish club was going to be the next big thing for me. Karen did very little to me at the club. She tugged on my nipple piercings a little, and she poured a pint of beer over me and got the slave of a friend of hers to lick the beer off me, but that was about all. Compared to some of the stuff I'd done at regular swingers' parties it was very tame. But I was really excited by it. When it came to the end of the night she asked me if there was anything else I wanted to do and I told her I still wanted to do loads more.'

Valerie and Karen exchange a glance. It would be romantic if not for the worry that Karen's attention isn't fixed entirely on her customer's tattoo.

'I'd seen people getting spanked and whipped in the club,' Valerie continues, 'and I'd been desperate to suffer that. Being chained to the wall had been good but I'd wanted more. Karen said more might happen next time. And then she took me back to her place and fucked me. And I've been genuinely hooked on the whole fetish scene from that point on. I happily dressed as Karen's slave, I've been whipped and spanked and nettled by Karen, and some of that has happened in front of people at her favourite clubs.'

Karen is now concentrating on the tattoo. Valerie watches her partner work and her expression is softened by genuine admiration and affection. 'I don't know if this is another fad,' she admits. 'Or if I've finally discovered what I've always been searching for. I will say that my longest previous fad lasted for about nine months. This interest in BDSM has now been going on for the best part of two years. I still think about the swinging clubs but I no longer think about going back to them. While I know there is lots of good sex to be found at a swingers' club I know it's nothing like what I'm enjoying with Karen on the fetish scene.'

Wendy is twenty-four years old: blonde, slender and very attractive. She is a single mother, lives in London and works as a model. Wendy swings irregularly, enjoying the freedom to attend parties and clubs with her occasional boyfriend Warren.

Wendy: 'I always tell people that I live for hardcore, but my definition of hardcore changes by the hour. Once I've done something, I stop thinking of it as hardcore.' Wendy shifts impatiently in her seat and seems to think she hasn't properly conveyed her point. 'When I go to a party I don't just want to see people fucking. That's something you'd see in the average person's bedroom. I want to see people getting whipped. I want to see and do things that properly shock me.'

When she receives a nod of understanding, she grins and continues. 'The most hardcore thing I've ever done was in a swingers' club up north. Warren had taken me there and, although it was a bit of a dull place, we livened it up when we arrived. I was wearing a leather mini-dress, thigh-high boots and a black leather dog collar. Warren waited until I'd gone to the bar to get our drinks, and then he started fucking me from behind. That's what I'd gone there for. Being pounded while I ordered the drinks; staring at the barman, a relief barman who wasn't into the scene and looked hilariously terrified by what was happening; I thought it seemed set to be a good evening. Then Warren started to pull on my dog collar.'

Wendy flashes a guilty smile. 'We'd tried choking games at home. But we'd never made them public before. He was riding me pretty well, I was certainly enjoying it, but when the lack of oxygen started to make me panic, that was when the excitement properly kicked in. Anoxia is a pretty extreme way to add something to sexual pleasure. When you're already at a swingers' party, and being fucked at the bar so everyone else can watch, it probably becomes very extreme. Which is probably why I got so much pleasure from it.' Wendy's smile remains fixed as an expression of guilt. But it is also obvious she is recounting a treasured memory.

'Yes, I fought Warren,' she agrees. 'I struggled to get him to stop. But secretly I wanted him to continue until I passed out. The party's host was nearby, smoking a cigarette with his wife and watching and he didn't say a thing. And Warren kept pulling the collar at my neck so the air in my lungs was getting less and less. Every sensation was more acute. Each time he pushed his cock into me I was enjoying pleasure I'd never experienced before. The whole situation was so intense that, when I came, the orgasm was sensational and I passed out.'

The light tone of Wendy's laughter should sit incongruously against an anecdote about being fucked into unconsciousness. But somehow Wendy has found a way to reconcile these two extremes.

'Warren told me afterwards that the party's host fucked me while I was unconscious on the floor,' Wendy adds. 'I don't approve of that. I usually insist on knowing who I'm fucking and deciding whether I want them or not. But I have to admit, every time I picture my unconscious body on the party floor, with some stranger sliding into me and fucking me, the thought gets me wet and horny again. Before I passed out, while Warren was still behind me, pulling on the collar and fucking me hard, I'd seen some people coming into the party. They'd pushed the door open, seen there was a woman getting fucked and choked at the bar, and then they'd turned straight round and not bothered to stay. It was their expressions of disgust and outrage that made me realise I'd achieved full hardcore shock status that evening.' Now there is no longer any trace of guilt in Wendy's expression. Her eyes sparkle with triumph.

'Not that it would have troubled me if I'd walked into a party and seen that happening. If I'd seen a woman getting fucked and choked at a bar when I walked into a party I would have thought, "This is my kind of place." But I don't think I'm the most extreme person out there. The catwoman we met at one of our first parties probably takes that prize.'

She leans forward when asked about the mysterious catwoman, clearly anxious to tell more. 'Me and Warren once went to a party that was proving to be quite slow. There was a bar, a few couples drinking and playing, but nothing much happening. They turned on some music and the catwoman, a friend of the host's, went on stage and started dancing. She'd been acting strange all evening. She was wearing a catsuit and had spent the night pretending to be a cat.'

Wendy shrugs, the gesture suggesting the catwoman's behaviour was eccentric, but not overtly remarkable. 'The catwoman was walking around the place on all fours, purring and licking people. That's why we called her the catwoman. I once did a similar thing to Warren. We'd been to a party and I had him on a lead and I said, "If you want a beer, you can have a beer, but it's being drunk out of this dog bowl." It was a fantastic turn-on. I really loved it. I ended up pissing in the bowl and made him drink it. It was great. Everyone in the room was watching him be my dog – on all fours – while he drank my piss from a bowl. It was a lot of fun.' She laughs when it's observed that, in that context, the behaviour of the catwoman seems neither extreme nor extraordinary and insists the woman was definitely extreme.

'We all got up to watch as the catwoman danced and stripped down to her heels and her PVC gloves,' Wendy explains. 'I was trying to get into the mood of the place but, aside from her being a bit peculiar, it was a little tame and unexciting. We were only staying because the place had a reputation for being hardcore but I hadn't seen anything to indicate it deserved that reputation. Then the catwoman announced loudly: "I'm going to fist myself." And I was thinking, "That's still not really hardcore." But I stayed and watched. And, while I'd expected her to fist her pussy, she got down on all fours and began to slide her fist into her arse.' Wendy laughs and says, 'That was when I started to become interested and impressed.'

Sitting forward again, gesturing with her hands to stress the point, Wendy says, 'I've never tried fisting but that's mainly because I don't want to try fisting. I don't mind what goes inside me but I want to be able to feel something else afterwards. I don't want my pussy to get like a bucket because I've had too many things that have overstretched me. The same rule definitely applies to my arse. I enjoy having things up there and I like to be able to feel them. But I want to be able to feel other things afterwards, and I'm sure fisting and overstretching would possibly have a long-term effect that I wouldn't want.

'But this woman on stage, this catwoman, she just touched herself for a moment and then slipped her hand all the way into her backside. I'm not even sure how she managed it. I assume she had lubricated herself before she began. And she must have been double-jointed or something. But she was pumping away and properly going for it. Getting a little bit deeper each time she pushed inside and eventually drove her arm in all the way up to her elbow.

'It was my first real shock of the evening. I was tugging at Warren's arm and saying, "Oh my God! How the hell is she doing this?" She was halfway inside herself. She looked like a contortionist. She looked like she was having an awful lot of fun. The grin on her face was pure contentment. And she just carried on and on pumping her arm backwards and forwards and getting deeper and deeper. When the music stopped she pulled her arm out dead quickly. She'd got something in her hand and she started doing exaggerated licks at her fingers and the stuff she was holding.'

Laughing, Wendy says, 'The whole room was in an uproar. There was one woman vomiting in a corner and everyone was shouting, "Gross!" and "Disgusting!" Everyone was going absolutely mental. And all the time this catwoman just continues to eat what she'd got in her hand and lick all the way up the sleeve of her long PVC glove.

'I spoke to her afterwards and she told us it had all been a stunt. The host had asked her to do something out of the ordinary for the party and so she put a bag of chocolate up her backside to provide a finale for her act. Of course, with the heat of being inside her the chocolate had melted. And, when it came out it looked like shit. But no one watching it knew that at the time.' She shakes her head. Wendy's admiration for the catwoman's stunt is obvious in her broad grin.

'After that the place got a deserved reputation for being really hardcore. I got Warren to take me there regularly. Personally, I have no interest in shit. I find it repulsive in a sexual context. But I do like the idea of shocking people and I love it when people are able to shock me. When I discovered the sort of people who were going there, very hardcore people, I decided I was definitely up for that.' Wendy is still smiling fondly when she says, 'I will always remember the catwoman just because she was so mental. And that's what I like to see. I don't want to see normal people. I want to be shocked. The catwoman embodied hardcore sex – admittedly in a bit of a grotesque way – but she still managed to excite and arouse me. I'd hate to have her as a friend because someone who goes to those lengths is clearly a fucking nutter. But the imagination, the thought process and the planning that went into her performance was awesome. And, while she's not a person I would pick for a friend, she's definitely the kind of person I would want to be hosting my parties.'

Mrs XXX is in her late twenties, married, and lives in the mainland UK. One of the conditions she imposed while we were discussing her swinging was that there would be no details included that could possibly lead to her identification. She accepted that she could be described as slender, dark-haired and attractive but didn't want any further personal information included.

Mrs XXX: 'You can write about this. But you have to change all the names and everything and you mustn't let XXX know about it because I've never told him and he's never going to find out.'

Mrs XXX waits until she hears the promise of absolute confidentiality, glances nervously around our private room, and then takes a deep breath to begin. 'Neither of us were virgins when we got married. But we weren't what you'd call worldly. We enjoyed sex, tried quite a lot of things, and then got stuck for other things to try. That was how we got into swapping at first, meeting other couples through contact ads, and then swinging at clubs and parties. We shared everything that happened, so there was no infidelity. If we did a separate-room swap I told XXX everything that I did with the other bloke and XXX told me everything that went on with him and the other woman. I don't know if it's really adultery if both of us knew what was happening. I just know we were always true to each other. Until I went and did the dirty behind XXX's back.'

Mrs XXX pauses and glances at the locked door of our room. She is blushing deeply. 'We were both at a club in [TOWN DELETED]. It was a place we'd visited half a dozen times before and we knew a few of the regulars. If we'd visited a couple more times we would probably have been called regulars too. We'd hooked up with this pleasant couple and the four of us had gone to a playroom. It was cosy, lit by a red light, and the whole evening had that raw sexiness I love at swingers' clubs. The music was loud, I could hear XXX and the woman he was with. They were moaning and groaning. The bloke I was with had been licking my pussy and getting me very wet. He pulled on a rubber and started stroking his cock against me and said, "Do you want this?"

'I told him to put it in me and he asked if I liked cock. I said I love cock and asked him to put it in me. He asked, "Is this enough cock for you?" and just kept stroking the end against my pussy. He asked if it was enough for me, or if I thought I could handle more. The teasing was driving me wild. Usually I prefer it when a bloke gets me wet and then rides me good and hard. This bloke was a real pussy-teaser, getting me wetter and wetter and making me more and more desperate. But, because I was enjoying the excitement of it, I played along for a while and let him tease me. He said a few other things, got me desperate for him, and then said, "I'll bet you'd love to do a greedy girl night." And that was when he finally pushed into me.'

Despite her nervousness, Mrs XXX smiles.

'While we were fucking he was talking all the time. It was good rude dirty talk. He asked me how I liked to be filled by different cocks. He asked me if I'd ever fantasised about being a greedy girl and he said I was the sort of cock-hungry slut who would probably enjoy having cock after cock after cock. I have to admit, he made me come very quick and very hard. XXX was still playing with the bloke's wife so I left the playroom and went to get a drink with the guy I'd been fucking. The conversation was still pretty rude between us and I asked him if he'd ever been to one of the greedy girl nights he'd been talking about. He said he went to them regularly and he was genuinely surprised that I'd never been to one. He told me about the last one he'd been to: two women and fourteen men. One of the women had been sitting in one of those swings they call a lover's seat. The other one had been bent over a table. He said that all of the men there had fucked both of the women at least once. The one in the swing just wanted cock in her pussy but the other woman wanted it everywhere. She had them in her mouth, between her tits, up her arse and in her hands, as well as filling her pussy. The bloke I was talking to really seemed to think I had the necessary "appetite" to enjoy one of those nights and he gave me his number so I could contact him if I was interested in doing one. By the time XXX and the bloke's wife joined us in the bar I'd heard enough about the greedy girl nights to know it was definitely what I wanted.'

Before she continues, Mrs XXX glances again at the locked door of our room. She is assured, if she doesn't want to talk about this subject she doesn't have to, but she seems determined to carry on. 'I told XXX while we driving home. He said no. I said a greedy girls' night sounded like fun, and reminded him that we'd got into swinging to try and stretch our boundaries, but he still said no. I was surprised he was so set against me going to a greedy girl night. From what I'd learnt, husbands and partners were always welcome, so it wasn't like he was going to be excluded. And I'd thought, since we were swinging to enhance each other's pleasure as well as our own, XXX would encourage me. But he just said a flat no and when I pushed him on the issue he said greedy girls were just cock-hungry sluts.' Mrs XXX smiles grimly and says, 'I wanted to tell him that I could be a cock-hungry slut when the mood took me, and he'd never complained about it before, but I could see he wasn't going to be swayed. And, at first, I thought it would be wisest to just forget about the idea. But, the more I tried not to think about it, the more I kept realising it was what I wanted. I like the atmosphere of swingers' clubs. And I love the electric tension of meeting a couple for a private swap. But the thing I love most is being filled with a stranger's cock. The idea of having as much cock as I could handle was too tempting. And, even though I'd never been unfaithful to XXX, the idea of being a greedy girl was more appealing than being a good and obedient wife.'

Mrs XXX sips at a glass of water. Her hand shakes slightly as she holds the glass but, again, she brushes aside the assurance that she doesn't have to continue if she doesn't want. 'I did bring the subject up a few more times before I planned to be unfaithful. I told XXX it was something I really wanted to try. I reminded him that we'd been to parties where I'd had four different cocks in one night, maybe eight or nine if you counted all the ones I'd stroked or touched, and I told him that I couldn't see that a greedy girl night was that much different to a full night at a swingers' club. But he was set on the idea that the whole greedy girl concept was wrong and every time I mentioned it, he just grew more and more adamant that it wasn't going to happen. So I did it behind his back.'

She pauses to reflect and then says, 'I think adultery is harder for swingers than it is for other people. We're all so used to being open and honest with our partners we don't know how to lie to them. Especially not about sex. I got in touch with the bloke who'd suggested I should do the greedy girl night, and I found out all the dates and times and everything. I then told XXX that my boss wanted me to attend an out-of-town business meeting. My company doesn't do many of those things, so it felt like a contrived story when I was telling XXX, but he didn't seem to suspect anything so I must have been fairly convincing. I then packed a small overnight bag, bought two large boxes of condoms, and went out to cheat on my husband with as many men as there would be at the party.' As she says this, Mrs XXX flashes a defiant smile.

'When I arrived the bloke I'd met at the party was there with his wife. They both made me feel welcome and we had a drink and got better acquainted before the party properly began. There were only a dozen guys there by the time they said the party should start and, even though I was a bit disappointed with the low turnout, I was told it was a pretty good result for midweek. The bloke I'd been chatting with seemed to be in charge of things and he suggested we start the night off with a show. I knew what this meant and me and his girlfriend started to dance and kiss and strip while everyone else was watching. It was fairly exciting. But it wasn't anything I hadn't done before. I usually had XXX somewhere nearby, watching and admiring. But him being absent was the only difference. We got down to our stockings and our thongs. The blokes watching were obviously quite appreciative, especially when she peeled the crotch of my thong to one side and started to go down on me. And I was quite worked up. So, when she stopped before she'd started, I thought it was a little bit frustrating. She turned to all these guys that were watching us and said, "I didn't come here tonight to eat pussy. I want some cock. Get your clothes off, boys, and show us your cocks." And none of them moved.'

For the first time in our interview, Mrs XXX laughs. 'I wasn't really surprised. Blokes are usually the last ones to undress at a party. But I did wonder how she was going to handle it. She winked at me then said, "The first bloke to get naked gets a BJ from both of us."' Still laughing, Mrs XXX says, 'You've never seen a dozen blokes race faster to get their kit off. We picked one bloke who had nearly injured himself leaping out of his clothes and, while she pinned him against the wall, I sucked and licked on his cock and his balls. Then I pinned him against the wall, squashing my boobs against him and kissing at his neck, while she went down on him. Eventually we both got to our knees and licked along his cock and his sac until the poor bugger couldn't hold it any longer. He spurted, shot half his load into my hair and the other half over her face, and that seemed to work like the starting gun for the rest of them.

'There were loads of hands all over us, clutching at tits, fingering pussies and everything. We were lifted up and carried to the table in the centre of the room. There were cushions on it, so it was fairly comfortable. I was laid on my back and she was placed on top of me so we were in a 69 position. With it being a greedy girl night, and with there being so much talk about all the cock that would be there, I hadn't expected to be facing a pussy for the night. But, because she was very good at sucking my clit, and because I got the pleasure of watching all the different cocks sliding in and out of her, I didn't complain.

'The bloke I'd been speaking with, the bloke who'd originally got me interested in the idea of becoming a greedy girl, said he wanted us in that position so we could keep each other safe. I think his exact words were, "You can both make sure no one goes in without wellies." But it didn't just mean we got to keep each other safe. She was licking and sucking on my clit while I was getting fucked. I was able to lick and suck at her as she took one cock after another. It was a good couple of hours. I think I got to have most of the blokes more than once, although I stopped keeping count eventually. The woman on top of me made sure I was constantly aroused, pushing her tongue into me whenever a cock slipped out and getting me wet in readiness for the next one. I repaid the favour at my end. It didn't matter that I couldn't see who was fucking me. The sensation of having cock after cock was what I'd gone there for and, on that score, the evening didn't disappoint. There was one period, about twenty minutes, where it was like I was locked in one long and constant orgasm. The pleasure was just rippling through me.' Softly, she adds, 'It's a shame XXX wasn't there to share the experience with me.

'It's not something I've done since and I don't think I ever will get round to doing it again. I've been on a big guilt trip ever since that night because I know, if XXX found out, he'd be very badly hurt. But I have to say it was very pleasurable. I'd wanted to try it and as it's satisfied my curiosity, I'm very glad that I did it.' She glances once more towards the locked door of our room and adds, 'If XXX ever comes round to my way of thinking, and decides that greedy girls aren't cock-hungry sluts in a bad way, I might get a chance to do it again one day.'

FEMALE SEEKS FEMALE

> **Female Seeks Female to** explore
> bisexual fantasy. Early 20s and seeking
> similar. No males or couples. Single
> females only. P.O. Box AL009

A close friend confided that one of the main problems of
being openly bisexual was the response it provoked from
other women. 'Half the women run away terrified, in case I
try and jump their bones. The other half try coming on to
me and then seem amazed that I don't want to fuck them
just because they're female.'

After appearing appropriately sympathetic, I asked about
those ratios and whether or not they suggested that fifty per
cent of her female acquaintances were either bisexual or at
least interested in experimenting with bisexuality. My friend
said she believed the figure was almost certainly higher, and
argued that many of those who ran away terrified were
possibly afraid of revealing a repressed interest in other
women.

Her rationale corresponded with my own observations of
swingers. Female bisexuality is commonplace within the
swinging community. Although there are some who argue

that women going with women is only pandering to male fantasies, many of the women interviewed for this book expressly stated that they were sexually interested in other women. Some had entered swinging because it provided an outlet for their bisexuality and allowed them to remain in an otherwise monogamous relationship. Even those who only experimented with bisexuality to appease an insistent male partner conceded that they wouldn't have done it if they hadn't harboured some degree of curiosity.

And the benefits of girl-on-girl action are constantly lauded. Women are reportedly better at oral sex than men. Women know how to touch another woman more ably than men. Women, women tell us, are simply better lovers than men.

Yet there still remains a large stumbling block for many women who want to explore their bisexual fantasies and have yet to find an appropriate partner. Visiting gay bars implies an enormous commitment to a lifestyle that might not be viable for the individual. Approaching likely friends and acquaintances seldom works successfully outside the pages of masturbatory fantasy. Swinging is one of the few ways in which a curious woman can safely explore her bisexual inclinations.

Many of the interviewees throughout this book have classified themselves as bisexual. Some of them are open about their interest in other women. Others keep the secret of their bisexuality confined to fellow swingers. The subjects in the following chapter focused expressly on the pleasures of women swinging with women.

Yvonne is twenty-eight and lives with a long-term partner of five years. She resides in Lincolnshire and works in education. Yvonne says she has tried being heterosexual and found it lacked a lot. She now considers herself bisexual on a 70:30 ratio with the majority of her sexual interest being for women.

Yvonne: 'I got into swinging via a fairly unusual route. I'd talked about fantasies with my partner at the time or, to be more exact, he'd asked me about my fantasies and I'd changed the subject to ask him about his. I wasn't willing to share my fantasies with him because I knew there was nothing he could do about them. He fancied the idea of swapping and watching and, although I was fairly cold to the prospect, I humoured him for a while.'

Communication with Yvonne has been mainly through email. This is our first meeting and she controls the conversation with businesslike efficiency. 'My partner's first suggestion – well, the first suggestion I accepted – was to visit him in an internet chatroom. I'd never done that before and what he was suggesting sounded like the tamest possible proposal. We'd both got laptops and a home network. He suggested we go on our laptops and visit the same chatroom, log in with unusual names, and see if we could find each other.' Yvonne sniffs sardonically and says, 'I thought it sounded like a good way to catch a computer virus and maybe waste an entire evening but, because he was so eager to try the idea, I figured I'd give it a shot just to keep him appeased.

'He took his laptop to the lounge and I took mine to the bedroom. He'd given me the website address for the chatroom and, because I wasn't that bothered about playing his game of virtual hide and seek, I signed in under my name.'

Yvonne grins sourly and says, 'I'd never been in an internet chatroom before and, logging into an adults only chatroom with a female name turned out to be a baptism of fire. Within five minutes I'd discovered so many things I suddenly felt like an authority. I could have gone on to *Mastermind* with internet chatrooms as my specialist subject. I'd learnt that most people don't have normal names: they call themselves things like Foot-long and Bi-girl and Cam-Guy. I discovered that PM means private message; that a private message is confidential and can't be seen in the main room; and that when you receive fifty PMs within one minute – and frantically try responding to them all – your laptop crashes.' She laughs at her own naïvety and then adds seriously, 'I also discovered that I got quite excited being propositioned by women and that was something I hadn't expected to discover in the chatroom.

'While I was trying to reboot the laptop my partner called up the stairs and asked me if I was in the chatroom yet. I called back and told him I was having computer problems but I'd be there in a minute.' Staring at the tape recorder as it catches her words, Yvonne says, 'The second time, when the screen asked me for my name, I called myself Girl4Girl. And that was all it took for me to discover my vocation in life.

'I'd occasionally hear my partner, shouting up the stairs and asking if I was the one he was chatting to. Most of the time I ignored him. I was busy talking to an American woman, Texas Rose, who was telling me about her experiences with other women. Until that moment I hadn't realised how much I wanted to try having a sexual relationship with a woman. But, as Rose described the sensations of going down on a woman, and explained how good women were with their fingers and tongues, I knew that was what I wanted – what I needed – to do.'

Yvonne confirms that the microphone will be able to hear her. She's lowered her voice as she talks about chatting with Texas Rose. When she's convinced that the microphone is recording effectively, she continues.

'I got really wet while she was talking to me. I explained that I'd never been with a woman but it had always been a private fantasy. I'd never dared do anything about the fantasy. I'd been scared to admit that I had such thoughts before but it seemed easy to talk about them to a stranger on the other side of a computer screen. She said, if we'd lived closer, she'd have introduced me to the experience. That comment got me shivering. Then we started chatting about what we were doing while we typed and she admitted she'd got a hand inside her panties.'

Sitting back in her chair, Yvonne draws a deep breath and laughs. 'I've found out since that not all women in chatrooms are genuine. A lot of the women are dickhead blokes pissing around and generally trying to get off by pretending to be someone they aren't. Afterwards I worried that Rose might not have been a woman. I've spoken to her a couple of times since and she always strikes me as one hundred per cent female. But, on that occasion, I didn't have any of those doubts or suspicions. I felt sure she was another woman. I also felt as though I was discovering what I'd been missing all my life.

'Rose explained to me that she was bisexual. She told me that women kiss differently to men: and not just on the mouth. She went into explicit detail about what she did with the last woman she went with and then explained that she and her husband often meet up with other couples so she can explore her bisexual side. When I asked her to tell me what that involved she said it was usually a night where she got to play with another woman while her husband and another man watched and whacked off.'

With a tiny sigh, Yvonne says, 'I have never before so wanted to live in Texas. I could have frigged myself to a climax chatting with Rose. I had one hand inside my panties and I could feel a special connection between me and this woman in the chatroom.

'My partner kept shouting up the stairs, asking me if I thought I'd found him yet, and I kept shouting back that I was still looking. He PM'd me a couple of times, not knowing it was me, I don't think, but I just ignored him. And I think I spent a good hour chatting with Rose on that first night. Well, I suppose we were doing more than chatting. I'm not usually one for playing with myself, which is all it was really. I was enjoying the sort of interactive porn that chatrooms provide. But the main point was that I was enjoying it and I was quickly coming to the decision that I wanted more. I finished chatting with Rose, touched myself until I came, and then went downstairs to find my partner. He'd just about given up on our game and seemed really surprised that I'd come downstairs in such a randy mood. I let him take advantage of that and told him the game had been arousing.

'We ended up playing the chatroom game every other night for a week or two after that. Each time I'd find myself having a long and wonderfully intimate conversation with a bisexual woman. And each of those conversations helped me find out more about myself.'

Still studying the tape recorder, Yvonne says, 'I've always found women attractive. Looking back, I think I've always found women more appealing than any man. But I'd never been able to accept that in my own mind. Talking on the internet allowed me to explore ideas I'd never properly considered before. I was talking to women who'd had sex with other women. They weren't ashamed or embarrassed about what they'd done. In the chatrooms most of them were quite proud of their accomplishments and eager to do lots more. It was exactly what I wanted.'

Yvonne sits straighter in her chair and says, 'I told my partner, if he could find me in the chatroom, I'd give him a special surprise. I hadn't said what that surprise was. I wasn't fully sure about it myself at the time. But, when I'd made up my mind, I responded to one of his PMs and said we should take it to the next level. He asked me what the next level was and I said I wanted to play with a woman. A real woman. The sex we had that night was the best of our entire relationship. He seemed surprised I was interested in women. I must have hidden it pretty well up to then.

'After that we were visiting the chatrooms every night looking for a woman who wanted to play with me while my partner was in attendance, or a couple with a woman like Texas Rose who would be happy for us girls to get together while the men simply watched and whacked off. We looked at other ways of organising what we wanted. My partner suggested we find a prostitute, which I vetoed straight away. From some of the discussions I'd had in the chatroom I'd learnt that I might get lucky in a private sauna. But swinging sounded like the most appropriate option. We checked out the various websites but I wasn't comfortable with them because the majority seemed to suggest that some sort of photograph would get the best results. My partner was comfortable with that but I didn't fancy having pictures of myself posted on the internet. About a month later, a month after I'd agreed to take it to the next level, my partner got us membership at a local swingers' club and I finally realised my fantasy.'

Yvonne finally takes her gaze away from the wheels of the tape recorder. 'I won't pretend it wasn't a nerve-racking experience. Even though I'd talked to hundreds of women in the chatrooms by that point, I still only had a vague idea of what to expect. I'd laid out very firm ground rules for my partner before we began. I told him that I was only interested in another woman – no men. I told him that nothing was going to happen unless I said it was going to happen. And I insisted, if I was uncomfortable or had a change of heart, I would be leaving straight away. He accepted all of my terms and, on that first night, we met Belinda and her husband.

'The hosts at the club were very good at their job. They were a personable couple who made us feel welcome, asked us what we were looking for and treated us as though we were special because it was our first time. When they heard I wanted to find a bisexual woman they promised they'd be able to introduce us to several couples who shared our interests. True to their word, before we'd settled down with a drink, we were in a conversation with Belinda and her husband and I realised I was dangerously close to getting off with a woman.

'Belinda was sexy and intelligent and I think she wanted me as badly as I wanted her. We chatted for a while and I noticed she was checking out my boobs and my legs. I'm used to that from men but it's not the sort of thing I've experienced from a woman before and it was an incredible turn-on. When I realised I was being eyed-up I could see that there, at the club, it was OK for me to do the same and check out Belinda's assets. She had a good figure, lovely legs, and a gorgeous pair of boobs. When she noticed I was looking at her figure she asked if we were just going to talk all night or if we were going to do something more. From there we went off to one of the playrooms, with my partner and her husband following behind, and I finally got to have sex with a woman.'

When asked about details, Yvonne demurely shakes her head. 'It was a wonderful experience – better than any sex I've ever had with a man. We're regulars at the club now and members at a couple of swinging websites. My partner is happy that our swinging allows me to explore my bisexual side and he gets to watch and wank while I have the pleasure of going with some very attractive women. I know it's not how every swinger swings but it's an arrangement that works very well for me.'

Zoe is forty-four years old and always maintained she was one hundred per cent heterosexual. She lives in London with two children and husband Zack. Zoe and Zack have been married for eight years and swinging together for four.

Zoe: 'I never really wanted to be into women. I'd always thought it was something of cliché. When we first started looking into swinging, talking about it, trying to find out whether or not we were serious, I always thought the girl-on-girl stuff was just fodder for sad male imaginations.'

Zoe puts a reassuring hand on my arm and insists that she hadn't meant any offence with the comment. We're talking outside her local swingers' club, close to the designated smokers' area at the rear of the building. It's a chilly night and Zoe has Zack's coat over her short skirt and strapless top to keep her warm.

'I didn't think the appeal of the girl-on-girl stuff was an outright lie,' she admits. 'I was sure there were lots of women who wanted to do it. But I also thought a lot of them had to be doing it because it was what their partners wanted and nothing to do with their own interests or arousal. And I insisted that women did nothing for me. Zack asked if I wasn't a tiny bit interested or a little tempted but I just told him he was subscribing to the myth of a male fantasy and that I didn't want to do anything sexual with another woman.'

A woman walks close to us and waves at Zoe. Zoe responds with a sly wink before returning to our conversation. 'I wasn't against women,' she says carefully. 'I could understand why Zack would point at the photo of one couple and say he found the woman attractive, and point at another and say that she wasn't his type. I could appreciate the aesthetics, but I just wouldn't accept that women might arouse or excite me.

'On one of our first times swinging we were with a couple and, although I'd stated that I wasn't bisexual, the woman was seriously interested in me. I felt bad because I thought she was a nice enough person, and fairly pretty for her age. But I had no sexual interest in her. I suppose the night would have been OK if she hadn't kept pressing the issue but she kept trying to tempt me into doing something and everything she said just hardened my resolve to have nothing to do with her. She said, "Do you want to kiss?"'

'I said, "No."'

'She said "Wouldn't you love to lick your husband's come from my pussy?"'

'I said, "No. But I'll probably be tormented by that image every time I try and lick the salad cream from the top of a crusty baguette."'

Zoe's grin can't be described as contrite, but she insists that she hadn't meant to be rude. 'The bluntness of that comment brought the evening to an abrupt end. They never got in touch with us afterwards and we didn't bother trying to organise a second night with them. Zack was a bit pissed that I'd been so rude but I'd tried to say a polite no and I was getting tired of having her shove her minge, metaphorically, in my face.' Zoe is still smiling as she adds, 'Not that there were many women like her. The majority of swingers we've met have been pretty cool about my limitations. If I say I'm not interested in women few people try and pressure me. And I never thought I was missing anything. Zack and I started off with couples, experimented with single guys for a few months, and then moved on to clubs like this one. We made it known that I had no interest in women and I think

I got a reputation for being something of a cock-addict. I did a couple of greedy girls' nights and I was usually the first woman to enter the playroom on an evening and the last one to leave.'

Zoe gestures to the main building of the swingers' club and says, 'It was here where we met Marcus and Madeline. We were all a similar age, got on well together, and had the same sense of standards and humour. Best of all, Madeline was exactly like me in that she wasn't interested in women. Her motto was: *If it's not got a cock, I can't fuck it*. We played with Marcus and Madeline at the club on more than one occasion and got to be good friends. Madeline's probably the woman I would now consider to be my best friend. It got to the stage where they would ring us before we set off to make sure we were going. On one night when Marcus wasn't able to go to the club, we took Madeline with us. It even got to the stage where they'd call round at ours for dinner on a weekend and –' Zoe exaggerates her tone '– most amazingly of all: we'd meet them sometimes and not have sex together.

'It was while they were round at ours having dinner one night that the subject got on to mine and Madeline's disinterest in other women. It was a regular topic of conversation. Marcus had said we were both attractive women. Zack had said he couldn't understand why neither of us had ever tried it. And Madeline said if they were so anxious to see some same-sex stuff going on, they should go fuck each other in front of a mirror. Marcus and Madeline had already heard about my licking-the-salad-cream-from-the-baguette comment, so they knew where I stood on this argument.'

Zoe's smile is softened with the recollection of a fond memory. 'It was a relaxed evening. The kids were about an hour in bed and safely asleep. We had no intentions of pairing off or playing as a foursome because it was a Sunday night and we all had work and school the following day. Also, Madeline is something of a screamer when she comes and we knew she'd wake the house if she started. I'd had a couple of glasses of wine, as had Marcus, but Madeline was sober so she could drive.

'Because she was sober, I was surprised to hear her suggestion. She said, if it was something Marcus and Zack wanted to see, she'd kiss me. She said, "If Zoe's up for it, you can both watch. And you can see that it's not a turn-on for either of us."' Zoe laughs as she says, 'You've never seen two men accept a suggestion so quickly.'

She shivers a little inside Zack's coat, although that's probably due to the cold night. 'I was a bit nervous,' she admits. 'I'd seen Madeline naked lots of times before and knew she had a very fit body. I'd seen her go down on Zack while Marcus took her from behind. I'd watched her with other guys at the club. And I'd had my hearing traumatised by the way she shrieks when she's coming. She's a very sexy woman but the idea of kissing her was something I'd never ever thought about. However, I figured it could help put an end to Marcus and Zack constantly urging us to do the bi thing. So I said yes. And that was what got me started into women.'

Zoe waves cheerfully at a couple who stand in the designated smoking area. They wave back and Zoe holds up a hand to indicate she will be with them in five minutes. Apologising for the distraction she says, 'We both stood up for the kiss. It was awkward in lots of ways, mostly because I hadn't prepared or anything. I was only dressed in jeans and a tee – not wearing my usual short skirt and stockings – and I had no idea how to kiss a woman who I thought of as my best friend. So we fumbled for a few minutes, trying to decide the best way to kiss each other. I was wondering where my hands and arms and legs and boobs should be when we kissed. Madeline was puckering up as though she'd never kissed a man or a woman before. I felt very self-conscious and I know I was as red as a tomato. Madeline looked equally embarrassed but she's the sort who, once she's said she's going to do something, she can never back down.'

With a small shrug, Zoe says, 'We went for it. Madeline was very gentle at first. I'd thought she was going to press her lips against mine and give me a hard, passionate, full-face kiss. Instead she was really light and tender. She had one hand on my hip and the other on my arm. I had a hand on her side, close to her boob but not touching, and my other hand was on the back of her head. It still strikes me as being strange that it was so arousing. We'd done lots of very raunchy things as a couple. With Marcus and Madeline in particular we'd been involved in some very erotic situations. Madeline and I had often been side by side on a bed while Marcus and Zack fucked us. I'd ribbed her for shrieking so loudly every time she came. We were already close and I thought we knew all of each other's erotic buttons. But, as it turned out, I didn't even know my own.

'It was a very exciting kiss.

'When we started to use our tongues on each other I already knew that I'd been missing out on something good. I think I touched Madeline's boob first, and found out her nipple was very stiff, and then we were pressing tight together and properly going for it. I did think of holding back. I'd spent so long telling myself that I had no interest in women that it was hard for me to accept I was kissing Madeline and loving the experience. But the more we got into it, the easier it was to forget that Marcus and Zack were watching and we just got caught up in the moment.

We ended up tearing the clothes away from each other. Madeline fingered me for a few minutes, I got my first taste of pussy, and then she was shrieking and Zack was running up the stairs to make sure the kids were OK. Madeline and me were both shaking and very surprised.'

The couple near the smoking area are waving for Zoe. She nods to tell them she won't be much longer. 'Marcus asked what it had been like and Madeline said, "Didn't I tell you? Neither of us are into women." That got us all laughing and we agreed, the next time we met up outside the club, we would meet at their place and see if we could take things further. We organised the date for the next weekend, and then had to cancel because it was the wrong time of the month for me. Madeline had to cancel the next one because it was the wrong time of the month for her and then our youngest got poorly so the week after that had to be cancelled too. Which was all bloody maddening and frustrating but we were used to delays like that. When the four of us finally did get together I was grateful that we had an existing friendship because otherwise I think it would have been very uncomfortable. Instead of me and Madeline getting straight down to what we'd all been waiting for, I paired off with Marcus and Madeline got intimate with Zack. After we were all satisfied and comfortable together, and with me and Madeline both being naked, it was easy to take things from there.'

Zoe has taken a step away now and it's obvious she wants to get to her friends and enjoy her evening. Before the tape recorder can be turned off she says, 'I had thought it was cliché. I hadn't thought I would ever find women sexually arousing. I would never have believed I could enjoy satisfying sex with a woman the same as I've enjoyed it with men. But Madeline proved me wrong several times that night. And I've had no qualms getting intimate with any other woman since. It was a revelatory night and it's changed the way Zack and I swing. He's more than content with the arrangement – I haven't yet met a man who doesn't want to watch his wife with another woman – and I'm happy that I've let myself discover this side to my nature. I also think that it's brought me closer to Madeline because, without her, I would never have tried anything with another woman. But, letting myself get intimate with another woman has brought a whole new dimension to our swinging experience.'

Abigail is thirty-four years old and lives near Derby. A part-time university lecturer, Abigail describes herself as currently single and mostly bisexual.

Abigail: 'My first ever sexual experience was with a woman. Well, a girl. We were both girls at the time. She was my best friend. We'd spend the night at each other's house. And our parents liked the fact that we were acting like protective sisters to each other. No one minded that we slept in the same bed when we stayed over with each other. And no one minded that we'd spend hours locked in the bedroom as we studied.' Abigail emphasises this last word with a wry smirk.

'The first sexual thing that happened between us was when we kissed. We'd slept naked with each other before, and I'd seen her develop into a young woman. But it was whilst we were talking about boys that we first became intimately involved. I'd been asked out by one of the boys at school and I'd told her I was worried about kissing him because I'd never done it before. She suggested we should practise and it turned into a very erotic experience for both of us. We didn't go all the way on that first time. But the following day, she caught up with me after school and asked me to say no to the boy who had asked me out. She said she couldn't bear the idea of me kissing someone else. Especially not a boy. I told her that I'd already blown him out. We went back to her house that night and did a lot more than kiss.'

We're sitting in a college refectory drinking unpleasant coffee. The mid-morning bustle is about an hour away and we're able to talk easily and without risk of being over-heard.

'As formative experiences go, it was a profound one with some long-reaching effects,' Abigail admits. 'I figured I was gay and acted and dressed accordingly. I found out about feminism at college and went on to do a degree in feminist theory. I stayed in touch with my first love even though we went to different colleges. We got together and stayed with each other as often as our schedules would allow until she turned up one day and said she was seeing a man.'

Abigail sucks her teeth. 'I have to admit I was hurt. But I eventually came to accept that it was her life and her choice and she could do whatever the hell she pleased. I tried being nice about it. I met him and he seemed pleasant enough, for a man, even though he was stealing my lover. She introduc-ed us and I could tell they were already close – patently sleeping together – and that upset me too. But I was grown-up about it, pretended we'd never had a relationship – because that was how she wanted to play it – and tried to carry on with my life.

'A month after I'd met him she phoned and said she'd had enough of men, missed me and wanted me. I saw her that night. We had sex. And then she went back to him the next day.'

Abigail's expression mixes frustration and admiration in equal parts. It's impossible to guess whether she was impressed by her lover's behaviour or incensed. 'Again, that was upsetting for me. It was confusing because I didn't know if we had a relationship or not. When she called me again, another month later, I saw her again, we both had a wonderful night, and then she went back to him. The third time it happened I told her that she was bisexual and needed to acknowledge that before she could feel settled in her relationship. She said I'd been reading too many college books. We had that same conversation a dozen times over the following year. Each time she called I was weak enough and desperate enough to give in and see her. Each time we'd spend a single night together and then she'd go back to being his painfully straight girlfriend for another month.'

Abigail giggles and says, 'I eventually told her she was treating me like a period. It was hard to have an argument about the subject because I didn't really want to upset her. She was having a hard time with the fact that she wanted to be the faithful and straight little wifey but she also wanted – needed – sex with another woman. I didn't want to make an issue of it because as long as she wanted another woman I knew she'd still be in my life. But, after a year, I could see she was upset with the whole situation and I told her she needed to do something.

'So she told him. She didn't tell him that she'd been seeing me since they first became an item. I don't think anyone, male or female, would have been happy to hear news like that. And I didn't think she needed to be so honest. But she explained to him that she was bisexual and told him that she'd been in a relationship with me before she met him. She said she wanted to be with him – she genuinely does love him – but she needed physical sexual contact with another woman.

'Typical man,' Abigail grunts with disdain. 'He said he wanted to watch. I said no. I said no at first but I was in an awkward situation. She'd done as I suggested and was trying to deal with the situation. And, although I didn't like the fact that he'd said he wanted to watch, when we spoke about it he didn't put it across like a typical man in the way that I'd expected. He said he wanted to watch because he loved her. He wanted to watch because, if her bisexuality was something that was important to her, he thought it was important that he share the experience with her. He admitted that the idea of watching two women together was a turn-on. But he also said he would respect any limits I imposed and, whatever happened, it would remain between the three of us.'

Abigail sips her coffee, sneers at the taste, and then says, 'I was still tempted to tell him to fuck off but I knew it was something my best friend dearly wanted so I agreed. The only condition I imposed was that I wanted to watch them first. I didn't really want to watch them when I made the suggestion. Being honest, the idea of seeing my girlfriend with her man made me feel physically ill. But I was trying to match his bravado and figured, if there was a way to make him change his mind, that could be a deciding factor.

'He said it was cool with him.

'And so, the next night, I went round to theirs and watched my girlfriend with her boyfriend. It surprised me that I found the night arousing. I'd seen pictures of naked men, and not been particularly impressed. But it was exciting to see one in the flesh, so to speak. It was also good to see my girlfriend enjoying herself. She looked horribly nervous when things began but she was satisfied by the end of the night and that was all that has ever mattered to me.

'They shared a bedsit. I was able to sit on one of the chairs in the kitchenette area of the room and watch as they pulled out the bed settee, undressed and then got down to the action. I'd be lying if I said I wasn't turned on. And I'd be lying if I said I didn't want to join in. But I was determined to impose some restrictions on what would happen in future and I wasn't going to do anything that would allow him to turn around and say, "Well you did such-and-such a thing . . ."'

Abigail gesticulates with one hand to show what she means and waits for my nod of understanding. 'I was excited watching his erection slide into her. We'd both played with dildoes when we were together, but dildoes are nothing like the real thing. Seeing his flesh go into her was acutely exciting. Watching her come – and she did come a couple of times – made me sure I was doing the right thing. But I just sat and watched on that first night and I had my first voyeuristic experience of heterosexual sex. My girlfriend seemed to get a lot out of it, so I couldn't complain about it on that level. And I did get aroused watching them. I was puzzled when I saw her sucking his cock, and apparently enjoying it. I couldn't understand what she was getting out of that. When I asked about it afterwards, she wasn't able to explain why it excited her. She just said it was a turn-on.

'So we agreed that he could watch me and her but I said there would be rules. I told him that he wasn't allowed to tell anyone, that he wasn't allowed to participate, and he definitely wasn't allowed to touch me. I made sure, when the three of us did get together, that I was looking irresistible for my girlfriend. I'd done the whole girly thing of buying sexy underwear, spending two hours in the bathroom doing my hair and stuff, and then wearing make-up and stockings and a skirt.' With a wry smile Abigail says, 'If I'd possessed a pair of heels I would have worn them.

'I was very self-conscious that first time.

'I was so used to being myself in the bedroom that I wasn't properly sure of how I should be acting or reacting with a third person there – especially when that third person was a man. But my girlfriend put me at my ease. Her boyfriend just sat on a chair in my bedroom, and eventually, when I was close to coming, I'd almost forgotten he was there. I half expected him to spoil the night by tugging off or asking if he could join in. But he was surprisingly understanding and sensitive. He let us get on with it, thanked me afterwards, and said it had been a genuine pleasure to see her being so fully satisfied. After that, it became a regular thing.

'Every other week the three of us would meet up for a drink or a meal. We'd either go back to mine or theirs, and I'd end up in bed with my girlfriend while her boyfriend sat beside the bed and watched. If I wasn't in the mood or it was my time of the month, I'd let them play together while I watched. And, one evening, when I was feeling particularly well disposed towards her boyfriend, I told him he could wank while he watched us, if that was what he wanted to do.

'We became a fairly regular trio and I could understand why she liked him, even though I was still a little awkward in his company. Nevertheless we both made an effort to be civil with each other and I chatted openly and honestly with him about sex whenever the subject came up. He seemed surprised that I'd never been with a man and asked if it was something I'd ever considered. I told him that I'd never given it much thought although, the more I watched him and her together, the more I did wonder what she was getting out of the experience. I'd been trying to imagine how it would feel to have an erection inside me. I said I'd been thinking of maybe picking a guy up and fucking him just so I could satisfy my own curiosity. He offered his services, with the proviso that it met with our mutual girlfriend's approval, and then neither of us did anything more about it for a couple of months. He didn't press the issue and I didn't go out of my way to raise the subject again because I didn't want to appear desperate.'

Abigail shifts closer and lowers her voice. 'It happened eventually. It was one of those nights when he was watching me with her. I invited him and had my first ever cock.' She's blushing deeply and it's difficult to decide if the memory is exciting or embarrassing. 'I can't say I felt as though I'd missed out on anything until I had a cock inside me but I could understand why she seemed to get so much pleasure from it. He didn't make me come. I don't think he was inside me for a minute before he was pulling out and spurting over my belly but, as brief as it was, it made me realise I could enjoy having a man inside me if I wanted.

'After that it was fairly regular for the three of us to end up in bed together. Most nights we stuck to the previous format of either me or him going with her. But we often ended up with all three of us in bed together and those nights began to become the norm rather than the exception. Almost always we were doing it for our girlfriend's pleasure. But there were times – his birthday was one occasion – when she and I would put on a girly show for him and then we'd all play. And there were times when they both went out of their way to make the night special for me. We were a triple for two and a half years before it ended.'

Smiling sadly, Abigail says, 'She got pregnant and decided she couldn't be a bisexual mother. I wanted to argue but I figured I would only be doing it for selfish reasons so I stepped away and our relationship now is purely platonic. I'm godmother to their daughter and I still see them both for meals and social things. I don't feel bitter because they taught me how to enjoy sex with men and women. I've been with other couples since and played with men and women. And, while that's proving to be a lot of fun, I still hope that one day my first girlfriend will call me and tell me she needs me again.'

LIFE-CHANGING EXPERIENCES

> **Curious Couple WLTM Similar.** M40
> F35. Both open minded and curious.
> We've heard a lot about swinging and
> want to find out more. P.O. Box AL010

Life-changing experiences can come in many shapes and forms. Not all of them are good and not all of them are the ones we want. In relation to this subject: swinging works for some couples and it doesn't work for others. Either way, it can prove to be a life-changing experience.

The majority of interviews in this book have come from women who positively endorse swinging, although it's usually with the proviso that it works for them but that doesn't mean it works for everyone. When swinging goes wrong it can be painfully destructive. Ill-prepared couples can be ripped apart; careless confidences can cost careers; and loving relationships can be buried beneath bitter memories. But, when swinging goes right, it can strengthen a marriage, support a sensational sex life, and rightfully earn its name as *the* lifestyle.

This last selection of interviews are from couples who have had their lives changed by swinging.

Beatrice is fifty-four years old and lives in the south-east. With her husband, Bob, she has been running a pub since the couple first met and married in their mid-twenties. The parents of three grown-up children and four grandchildren, Beatrice and Bob claim they have been 'officially' swinging for about ten or twelve years, although they admit they might have been doing it 'unofficially' for a lot longer.

Beatrice: 'I think we'd been having sex with other couples for about five years before we realised we were swingers. Back in those days it was called having an open marriage and me and Bob were fairly honest about who we were going with and what we would be doing with them. I'd been with several of the regulars from the pub. Bob had been with lots of the barmaids and he'd played with a couple of our mutual friends. It was never cheating because we both knew what the other was doing. I told Bob all about the men I was seeing and he didn't hide any details about his girlfriends and what they got up to from me. We talked about it, shared the experiences, and shared each other's excitement. When we first found ourselves having sex with another couple at the same time that just seemed like a natural extension of what we'd always been doing.'

Beatrice has suggested our interview would be best carried out in a room above the pub. From below the sounds of a busy weekend are still loud enough to interfere with the recording levels on the tape recorder. Bob is now running the pub without his wife's help but Beatrice insists he is 'big enough and ugly enough to manage on his own'. While we try to find somewhere appropriate for the microphone, Beatrice produces a large photo album marked PRIVATE and shows off a series of saucy pictures that reveal her with Bob and others.

'I can't say that it's changed our lives, because it's always been a part of our lives. When we first started seeing each other, and this would be back in the early seventies, we got together under the tacit agreement that we could still see – still have sex with – other people. Bob knew that I was going with his brother and an old on-again-off-again boyfriend while we were first dating. I knew he was knocking off a couple of lasses on the delivery round he had back then. When he gave me an engagement ring and proposed marriage the first thing I said was, "This isn't going to mean that I have to stop screwing other people, is it?" He laughed and said, as long as he didn't have to stop, I could carry on screwing whoever the hell I wanted.'

Beatrice's laugh rings merrily around the room. She is still leafing through the photo album, pointing out pictures of particular interest and commenting on what the evening of each photograph involved.

'It worked out to be the best arrangement possible for us. We were always discreet about what we did and who we saw. I'd tell him, "Oh! I might not be back until very late tonight," and he'd say, "Well make sure you tell me all the dirty details as soon as you get back." Or he'd say to me, "I'm going to make sure one of the barmaids gets home safe tonight," and I'd say, "Fill me in on what you get up to," and we'd both laugh and know that the other was going to be screwing someone else.

'We ended up screwing another couple without planning. They were both new to the pub, I'd been working behind the bar and chatting with them, and Bob kept coming over and exchanging pleasantries. When it got to chucking out time Bob asked them if they fancied staying for another and they were both up for it. Bob saw the last of the customers out of the door and locked up. I went to get us all fresh drinks and, when I got back to the table, Bob was kissing this woman and had his hand inside her blouse. Her husband was just sat watching them, smiling a little, but not doing anything about it. I watched them for a minute and then said to her husband, "Should we show them how it's done properly?"

She laughs again and the sound is infectious. It would be patronising to describe Beatrice as larger than life – the description is usually only used for women who are a size 18 or above – but her presence fills the room.

'He had me across the table,' she continues. 'Bob took her over the bar. She said it had always been a fantasy of hers to be ridden over a bar while she held a pump in each hand. I couldn't understand why that was a fantasy anyone would ever have but I was pleased that Bob was able to fulfil her needs. They screwed each other afterwards – she insisted that her husband take her over the bar again, with a pump in each hand – and Bob gave me one at the same time.'

Still chuckling, Beatrice says, 'I remember that night, not just because it was the first time we'd ever swapped with another couple, but also because of what Bob said while we were screwing. He was taking me from behind, he had his face pressed against the side of my neck, and he was whispering that I'd looked beautiful with another man's dick in my chuff. I could tell he was excited. His dick was harder than usual and he seemed more frantic in the way he was screwing me. And when he kept telling me how much he'd enjoyed seeing another man's dick in my chuff, I saw that we both enjoyed seeing each other with other people. We screwed the other couple again before the night was over. Then we chucked them out of the pub, went off to bed, slept, and screwed each other again the following morning.

'It wasn't a conscious decision, I don't think. I can't remember us sitting down and having a full-blown conversation about it. But from then on we both seemed to be looking for other couples we could play with rather than just meeting up with people on our own.'

Unexpectedly, Beatrice takes the photo album away. She replaces it with another that has no title and winks as she says this is the one to look at. The previous album had shown pictures of Bob and Beatrice with other couples, mostly clothed pictures, many of them suggestive because of their poses. The photographs in this album are far more explicit.

'It wasn't easy finding other couples. I got chatting to one of the blokes I'd seen a few times. We'd just had sex and I asked him if his wife would be up for playing as part of a foursome. He looked at me in disgust and said, "Of course she bloody wouldn't. What do you think she is? A pervert?"' Beatrice shakes her head to dismiss him. 'But me and Bob did all right. With owning a pub we were in the right place and because we were working together we could usually get each other's opinion straight away. Bob would point out a couple and ask me if I thought they were game. I'd weigh them up and, usually, I'd agree that there was a possibility. He's got a good eye for likely couples and I think he's been right more often than he's been wrong.

'So I'd go and chat with them, just being friendly and maybe being a bit flirty, and if it turned out they were up for it, I'd ask them if they fancied staying behind for a swift one after chucking-out time. You'd be surprised by how many women want to be taken over a bar while they're clutching a beer pump in each hand. I've tried it myself,' Beatrice admits, 'but I can't see the appeal.

'Sometimes a couple would come back to see us again. Well, that happened quite a lot, actually. If I was serving and I saw them, I'd go through to the back and tell Bob, "Dick and Jane are here again." And he'd say, "Do you fancy asking them to stay after hours?" And then we'd be at it again until the early hours.

'Anyway, we'd been doing that for about a year when one of the couples we'd seen a few times mentioned swinging.

They'd been looking to meet up with other couples, they'd actually been trying to meet up with another couple on the night we first met them, but their date turned out to be no-shows. And they asked us which swinging contacts mag we used. Bob looked puzzled by the question. I told them we weren't swingers. And they pointed out that we regularly screwed other couples and they wondered what we would call that if it wasn't swinging. Which made perfect sense as a question, I suppose.'

The photographs in the untitled album show Beatrice and Bob naked. Some of the photographs show Beatrice with other men and others show Bob with other women. The sexual content in each picture is explicit. Beatrice is shown naked and performing fellatio. Bob is shown behind a busty blonde on all fours. Another photograph shows Beatrice holding a thick hard erection in each hand. Beatrice laughs at this one and says, 'I can't tell you what happened that night. That was really rude.'

Getting back to the subject of her introduction to swinging, she says, 'Since we'd started going with other couples both me and Bob had cut down on the single people we saw until that had almost stopped happening. I knew that Bob still screwed the occasional barmaid but we seemed to spend more time trying to get with other couples so we could be together when we were screwing other people. It was always fun to hear about what he'd done with another woman. And it was always exciting to tell him what I'd done with another man. But it was far more satisfying to see everything as it happened.

'Chatting with the couple who identified us as swingers, they told us about some of the clubs they had visited and said we should join them the next time we fancied a night away from the pub. They spun such exciting tales about playrooms, group stuff and orgies that Bob wanted us to close the pub and reopen it as a swingers' bar in the morning. Of course, I told him to be a little more patient, but I shared his enthusiasm to find out what we'd been missing.'

Proudly, Beatrice takes the photo album and flicks through to a section near the back. The picture shows Beatrice's face, sweated with semen, with at least five penises pointing at her. She's grinning broadly in the picture. Glancing up from the picture, it's observed that Beatrice wears the same broad smile in most circumstances.

'We never did turn the pub into a swingers' club,' Beatrice admits. 'Although Bob keeps saying that's what he plans to do one day. But we did find a new way for us to spend our free time. The other couple took us in and got us settled. Even though we'd been used to going with other couples and enjoying an open marriage we were both a little bit daunted by entering a swingers' club. It didn't take long for us to be put at our ease. The couple that had taken us there showed us around, introduced us to the owner, and by the end of the night we were as settled there as we would have been here. Bob got us talking with a very attractive couple and I ended up going down on a woman – which was a first for me. The whole experience was a real eye-opener. We'd both been open about our enjoyment of sex since we met and married but we'd never encountered a group of people who shared our attitudes. Which is why I'd say that it wasn't swinging that changed our lives: it was discovering other swingers.'

Caroline is forty-five years old and lives with Craig in southern Scotland. The mother of three children, Caroline and Craig tried swinging after the last of their children had grown up and moved away from home.

Caroline: 'Swinging definitely changed our lives. We had a good sex life when we first met but it was never anything special. Craig was always satisfied but I have to admit I was often left frustrated. I attributed a lot of that to being tired. We had children early on and they were always a handful. If I'd spent a full day running round after them, as well as doing all the stuff in the house and my part-time job at the library, I was exhausted by bedtime and I invariably looked run down. By the time I crawled into bed I usually wasn't fit for anything except going to sleep. I often said, if Craig wanted sex, he could go ahead as long as he didn't wake me.'

Caroline chuckles. It's hard to imagine the woman she's describing because Caroline looks far from tired. When she shows family photographs of those days the effect is peculiar. The woman she was back then has dark circles under her eyes and is dressed for comfort rather than fashion. If Caroline wasn't adamant that pictures show her, it would be easy to believe she is pointing to the image of an older and less glamorous sister.

'It carried on like that for a long time,' Caroline explains. 'We fell out of the habit of doing it and never really fell back into the habit until a lot later. The eldest had left home the year before. Our daughter had moved in with her fella, and our youngest was talking about joining the army. I'd gone from being a full-time parent and part-time librarian to being a part-time librarian with a lot of spare time on my hands. I asked for extra hours at work, and got them. I went to lots of work social dos, leaving parties, hen nights and girls'nights, and I listened to so much talk about sex I began to wonder what I'd been missing. I eventually plucked up all of my courage and asked Craig why we weren't having sex any more. He said he'd been wondering the same thing himself for some time.'

She lowers her voice to a confidential whisper and says, 'So we tried it again and found that it was fun but we both knew it could be better. We dosed Craig up with Viagra and that helped a little, but not as much as I'd hoped. Whatever we did, I always felt as though it could have been different. More exciting. Better. Craig was very understanding and he kept asking what he could do to improve things. I considered the question seriously and told him it would help if we were doing something more daring. He wanted to know what sort of thing I would consider daring and I said I had no idea. I just felt as though what we were doing wasn't very exciting.'

Caroline sits back in her seat and muses philosophically, 'I suppose part of that was because we'd been having sex fairly young. Not illegally young, but we'd been together from the age of seventeen and fallen into the sexual rut of being tired parents before we'd reached twenty. Consequently, with us spending a further twenty years not doing much sexually and devoting our time to kids and work, everything we did either seemed overrated or a bit on the dull side.

'Craig surfed the net a little bit – we did that together – trying to find something that sparked our interest or made one of us get excited. But he kept coming up blank. We talked about me wearing exotic lingerie, or both of us wearing rubber or leather, but we both knew, if we did those sorts of things, it would still be just him and me but wearing different clothes. Bondage didn't appeal to either of us. It's too cold up here to do anything outdoors. And neither of us wanted to hurt each other with whips or paddles. I suppose we latched on to the idea of swinging out of pure desperation.'

Caroline smiles and says, 'I wasn't particularly excited by the idea of swinging at first. I agreed to the suggestion because it sounded better than us simply dressing up or weeing on each other. And I knew, if we didn't pick one of those choices, it looked like we'd practically run out of options. I figured we could try swinging and if it didn't work – and I didn't expect it to work out – I could always go and get myself a membership card for the local bingo and take up knitting or crocheting or something.

'Not that I knew much about swinging before we began. I had an idea that it was something to do with putting car keys in a bowl. My vague idea was that I'd be expected to bonk another man while Craig got to bonk another woman. I figured I could put up with someone bonking me for half an hour – taking one for the team, as they say – whether it worked out to our satisfaction or not.'

Again, Caroline appears philosophical as she says, 'I thought jealousy might be something of an issue for Craig. He's always been a very manly man and I didn't think he'd be happy about the idea of another man bonking his wife, but he was fairly relaxed about the prospect. He said, with the situation as it was, we were both getting jealous of everyone else in the world with the perfect sex lives that we imagined they had. If swinging helped us get what we wanted then he had more reasons to be grateful to it than be jealous because of it.

'Which made sense to me.

'Craig asked if I wanted to try a club first, or meet another couple. I said a club because – and this sounds stupid in retrospect but it is the truth and it probably shows how naïve I was – I said a club because I couldn't understand the point of swapping car keys if there was only one other couple there.'

Caroline's chuckle is rich with self-deprecatory humour. The fact that she is not embarrassed to admit she was unworldly when she entered swinging makes her insights seem somehow more honest.

'We found the address for a club online. There were a couple of places closer but I thought, if we travelled a bit further out, there was less chance of Craig bumping into anyone he knew or me meeting anyone who could recognise me from the library. Craig took care of all the arrangements, phoning them up and finding out the best night for us to attend and asking about dress codes and that sort of thing. And, for the first time in two decades, I began to get very sexually excited. It was September and Craig had planned for us to go in the October.

'We know now that there's no real need to book so far in advance, but Craig had wanted to give me time to think about it and change my mind if necessary. I'd wanted to make sure I'd thought of everything and prepared myself properly before we went there.'

Again, Caroline discreetly lowers her voice to talk about sex. 'In the weeks before we went I found myself getting excited every time I thought about going to the swingers' club.' She knowingly nods towards her lap and whispers, 'I'd think about it when we went to bed and then bonk Craig rigid while we talked about the sorts of things that might happen. For the first time in two decades I was actually touching myself when Craig wasn't around. I even went out and bought a vibrator. I still had an idea that car keys might be involved somewhere, although we'd read enough online to be aware that my interpretation of events was possibly a little on the wrong side.

'And then I began to have second thoughts.'

Settling back in her chair she says, 'I told myself that the fantasy had been good while it lasted, but that the reality was likely to be a major disappointment. We were likely risking twenty plus years of marriage for a stupid idea that probably wouldn't be half as good as I was hoping. But I think that was what made me decide to go. I figured, if our marriage was going to continue to be dull and sexless and uninteresting, then it wasn't much of a thing to risk losing. I love Craig immensely. But our life together was incredibly dull and, as selfish as it sounds, I needed more.'

Caroline looks painfully earnest as she says, 'I'd spent twenty years being a good wife and a good mother and now it was time for me to have something for myself. So we went. The swingers' club was nothing like what I'd been expecting. No one asked for our car keys. The hosts were used to virgins like us and they took us round the place, showing us the playrooms and the private rooms, explaining what was allowed and what wasn't allowed, and then sitting us down to chat about what we wanted from the club. They really put us at our ease and that wasn't an easy task. As soon as they had said they were swingers I was expecting him to say to me, "Get your knickers off and let's have a bonk." But they put no pressure on us at all. In fact, they advised us not to do anything on our first couple of visits except enjoy the atmosphere and chat with a few couples and get to know people. And while it seemed like the stupidest advice ever from the host of a swingers' club – come a few times and don't have sex – that lack of pressure was just what we needed. It allowed us to learn what happened at the club and it allowed me and Craig to find out what we wanted from swinging.'

We discuss the club briefly and other local venues in the area. Caroline and Craig have tried to remain loyal to the first club they visited but the appeal of different clubs with different customers has made them familiar with most of the local swingers' clubs.

'We were tempted to do more on that first night,' Caroline admits. 'The first couple we chatted with wanted us to join them in one of the private rooms. But we said we were still finding our feet and they were sympathetic and understanding. We must have spent an hour talking with them, talking about sex and what we liked and what we wanted. Then they went off and hooked up with another couple and I was thinking, *The next time we meet them, the four of us will end up together and it will be bloody good.* I think, it was when that thought went through my mind, I realised that swinging was exactly what we needed in our lives. I don't think we've ever seriously looked back and regretted the decision since. And I don't think we ever will.

'It's not all been plain sailing,' Caroline admits. 'We've had arguments. Craig's acted like an inconsiderate bastard and I've behaved like a selfish bitch. But the arguments don't come very often and I think arguing is good because it means we've got some sort of passion between us and we didn't seem to have that when we were bringing up the kids.'

She raises her hand to interrupt herself, suddenly remembering an important anecdote. 'I bumped into a friend recently. She was the mother of a kid who used to be at school with our eldest. She was really amazed when she saw me because she said I looked so much better than the last time we'd bumped into each other in a school playground. She said I looked so much younger. I would never have told her my secret – I don't talk about swinging with anyone outside the club – but I know why I'm looking so much better these days. It's all down to the fact that swinging has really changed my life.'

Dorothy is thirty-two years old and lives within commuting distance of central London. She has been swinging for six years and knows it is the perfect lifestyle for her and her Hubby. In her contact adverts she describes herself as a size 8: bubbly blonde.

Dorothy: 'It's certainly changed our lives. To be honest, swinging *is* our lives. We wake up on a morning and we chat about couples and parties over breakfast. Hubby works in the city, so he's off early but we always have an intimate kiss and cuddle before he leaves. I'll spend the day answering emails, checking our ad and doing wifely things. Then, when he gets home, we have a quick meal and talk about what we want to do with the evening.'

Dorothy is only wearing underwear as she speaks. She sits in her lounge, in front of an open laptop, and toys absently with the webcam. She explains that she's in the middle of getting ready to go out and asks if it's OK for her to continue getting ready while we chat.

'Midweek is one of the best times to organise a threeway,' Dorothy continues, referring to her usual schedule. 'If I haven't set something up by the time Hubby gets home, he'll join me on the net and we'll surf a couple of chatrooms until we find a suitable guy. If we're all up for it,' she smiles and adds, 'and Hubby and I are almost always up for it, then we'll meet and fuck.' Grinning lewdly she says, 'After that Hubby and I go home, fuck again, and then sleep to repeat the routine the following day.'

Our conversation is interrupted as Dorothy replies to someone in a chatroom. Multitasking, she is getting ready for a night out, talking to one of the men she might be seeing this evening, as well as participating in our interview. 'This one's acting like a bit of a tosser,' she mumbles as she types. 'And I'm betting he'll be a no-show. I've just asked him to turn on his cam and show me what he's bringing tonight but he's messing me about.' She gestures towards the laptop screen and indicates the webcam image of a man's crotch. She is still typing and, when she presses the return key, the image of a crotch moves slightly. Hands appear and unfasten a zip and the image onscreen now shows a disquietingly large erection. Dorothy types 'mmm-mmmmmm' and then presses return. Turning away from the laptop she says, 'I hope he does turn up tonight. That looks serviceable.'

Alternating between our interview and the online conversation she says, 'We don't go swinging every night. There are a couple of days each month when I'm not up for it. And there are plenty of times when our third man proves to be a no-show. But most week nights we have some sort of swinging fun and, if we're not actually with another person, we're usually talking about it or plotting and planning.'

Still multitasking, Dorothy shifts the position of her chair and switches her cam on. She waggles her chest at the webcam and then pulls one cup of her bra down to flash a glimpse of nipple to her online correspondent. Rearranging the cup and concealing herself she smiles tightly and says, 'That's as much as he's getting for now.' Turning away from the laptop, she comments on the madness of doing so many things at once and disappears from the room to retrieve a dress.

From the other side of the door she calls, 'Weekends are different from this sort of thing. We save weekends for clubs and couples. Friday and Saturday nights are spent at one or the other of our regular clubs and, if we've not organised anything for the Sunday, Hubby will take us to a club again then.' When she gets back into the room she is wearing a sleek black mini-dress. The underwear she had been wearing is now in her hand. Sitting down in front of the laptop she finishes her conversation and tells her online friend that she will see him soon.

'Yes,' Dorothy admits, 'we are obsessive about our swinging. Everything we do is swinging. When I buy clothes I'm wondering how they'll look at the club or when I'm on a date. When I go out anywhere I'm eyeing up strangers, wondering if the couples might be players, or wondering if a particularly attractive woman could be bi-curious.' Laughing softly as she uncrosses her legs and slips into a pair of heels, Dorothy says, 'When Hubby and I go out as a couple we both act like we're single. We're forever flirting with other singles, just to see how far we can push things. Swinging is our lives.'

Through an exchange of emails we've already discussed Dorothy and her partner's swinging preferences. They both enjoy clubs. Dorothy says she likes threesomes best because she enjoys being the centre of attention. Both Dorothy and her partner are bisexual which, she says, makes the threesomes satisfying for all concerned.

'It helps that we met through swinging,' Dorothy informs me. 'I was in a semi-serious relationship that was going downhill. He suggested swinging as a last resort to try and stop us from losing what we had. Hubby was in the same situation and, when we met at a party, we realised we had more in common with each other than we had with our existing partners.' Her expression is torn between a natural cheerfulness and the obvious upset of this memory. 'While it was sad for our partners, I think it's turned out best for all in the long term. I'm sure my ex didn't want to be burdened with a slut for a partner. And I know Hubby's first wife wouldn't have been happy if he'd continued to fuck around behind her back.'

Dorothy leads us through to her bedroom so she can apply make-up before leaving to meet her date for the evening. She explains that she's agreed to meet her Hubby and the man she had been chatting with at a bar that's not too far away. It means her husband can make an early start on the evening, because the location is on his journey home, and Dorothy says it's the ideal spot for finding an alternative partner if the online date disappoints in any way.

Multitasking again, Dorothy explains all this while chatting on her mobile to her beloved Hubby.

'Perhaps that's the reason why we get so much out of it?' Dorothy suggests. 'We both love each other, deeply and immensely. But we also both love sex. Neither of us is troubled about the other being with someone else. I like the fact that Hubby is having sex with other men and women because that means he's being satisfied. He's said he feels the same way about me.' Dorothy falls silent as she applies lip-gloss. When she speaks again it's clear that she's been considering her previous comments. 'I don't think we need the swinging as a couple. I think we could get along without it if one of us ever decided we'd had enough. But I can't imagine that ever becoming the case because, for us, it's our way of life.'

FINAL WORDS

Author Needs To Thank contributors, editor, spouse and readers. You all know who you are. And you all know I'm in your debt. THANK YOU. P.O. Box AL011

The preceding pages have attempted to address the original question: *Why do women swing?* In some ways I think the question has been answered. In other ways I think more questions have been raised. The whole subject is a little like unravelling Christmas lights: once you think you've untangled an entire thread, you end up with four more leads in your hands, each one twisted and leading to another bundle of knotted complications. So, rather than trying to summarise all that has been said, I asked each of my interviewees to sum up their thoughts on the subject in a few short words. The question I asked each woman was simply: why do you swing?

Amy: *I do it because I like sex. I enjoy making love to my husband. But I like the adventure of having sex with different partners. I do it for that reason and because it* *satisfies something inside me and because it gives pleasure to me and my husband.*

Beryl: *We do it because it's so much fun.*

Chelsea: *I like sex. I go to the parties because they give me what I want – what I like. One day I'll probably give them up, if I ever meet a man who I think I could settle down with – a man who satisfies all my needs and makes me want him and no one else. But, until he comes along, I'm going to continue going to the parties.*

Darla: *I've always done it. Sometimes I like cock and sometimes I like pussy. I can get both at a swingers' club, or I can get whichever I want.*

Eliza: *I do it to earn £1,000.*

Fiona: *Swinging enhances our relationship. It's not something we have to do. But it's something that we really enjoy doing. It keeps our relationship exciting and, because we met knowing that's what we like to do, it's just become part of us.*

Gloria: *We do it because it's made our sex life better. It was good before. But it's new and improved now. Everyone does sex differently and it's like a sexual learning experience. It's certainly made me more aware of how to satisfy my husband, and I know it's made him more aware of how to satisfy me.*

Helen: *I did it because it seemed like it would be fun and different. It was fun, but the upset afterwards was devastating. I don't think I'll be doing it again because I don't think*

I'd want to risk suffering that hurt again. If everyone in the world was honest and didn't cheat and lie I'd be tempted to try it a second time. But I don't live in that world.

Isobel: *We do it because it's satisfying. If Iain decided, for some reason, that he didn't want to do it any more, I would be upset, but it wouldn't spoil our relationship. I think it would be the same if I got tired of the meetings that don't work out.*

Joyce: *I like to be admired. I like sex. And I like to think that men are being aroused by me, whether it's my photograph or the real thing. I do it because it lets me know that I'm attractive and exciting.*

Kara: *I do it for the DPs.*

Lorraine: *We do it because we're able to. We've always enjoyed sex. We spent twenty years looking after the kids and living our lives for them. Now they've grown up and moved on it's time for us to start having fun. We're not hurting anyone (unless they ask us to) and we're having a lot of good, adult fun. We do it for the simple pleasure of doing it.*

Maria: *I do it for the cock.*

Nadine: *It's fun and exciting and I can't see a down side. I get the arousal when I plan an evening with Nigel. I get the arousal from the evening itself. And I get a sense of satisfaction from being so grown-up about my sex life. I know that what we do is unconventional and I feel as though I'm being adventurous by doing something unconventional.*

Olive: *I don't think of it as swinging, although I suppose that's what it is. I go to the parties because it's exciting and fun. I go so I can experience having sex and being desired by a man other than my husband. But mainly I go to feel young.*

Penny: *I did it because I enjoyed the atmosphere of dogging. Once I've worked out a way to do it safely in the future I'll be doing it again. But I'm not doing anything until I can be sure it's one hundred per cent safe.*

Kylie: *It's become a way of life for us now. We swing because we like having sex. We like being around people who are comfortable talking about sex. And we like the relaxed atmosphere of being with people who aren't shocked or embarrassed by our lifestyle.*

Rosie: *I guess I was lucky to find Robert. I'm kinky and he's supportive of that. Like I said before, I think women's bodies are built to be pleasured by more than one man and I think the happiest and most satisfied women are those who act on that knowledge. I do it to be a happy and satisfied woman.*

Sonia: *The orgies are by far the best part. Being in a bed with a dozen other naked strangers has to be the hottest thing anyone could ever experience. If that was the only thing swinging had to offer me, I'd do it for that alone. But because there's so much more, I do it for all that as well.*

Tiffany: *It feels like something we've always done. It's hard to say why we do it. I do it because it makes me feel attractive and desirable and alive. I suppose, as soon as it stops making me feel all those things, I'm going to stop doing it.*

Uma: *I do it because it enhances my sex life. The sex I had with my husband was always pretty good. But the sex we've had since becoming swingers has been tremendous. It seems to have brought us closer together and made some stuff that was already exciting a lot more exciting.*

Valerie: *I can't think of anything else I would rather do. Whether it's swinging, going to a fetish club, or just being involved in a group thing, being involved in sex is exciting for me and it's what I live for. I do it because I can't imagine not doing it.*

Wendy: *I'd have to say I do it for the hardcore. I have a very demanding libido and I like to be shocked and surprised. Swinging doesn't just allow me to be shocked and surprised. It also lets me be close to people who are fairly comfortable with those levels of shock and surprise. As long as I'm hanging around with members of the swinging community I know I'm in for a few pleasant surprises.*

Mrs XXX: *We swing because it's a lot of fun and I think it does bring us closer as a couple. I have done the occasional thing that my husband doesn't know about, and I think our marriage is going to be a happier one if I keep those secrets from him. But on the whole, we swing because it's fun and naughty and satisfying.*

Yvonne: *I do it so I've got a chance to have sex with women. I enjoy sex with men. My partner satisfies me and I'm happy with him. But I get a lot of pleasure from having sex with women and swinging allows me access to that pleasure.*

Zoe: *I like sex. Swinging allows me to enjoy lots of sex with lots of different partners, but at the same time have the trust* *and companionship of my husband and my best friend. It works perfectly for me.*

Abigail: *I'm bisexual. Going with couples is a way for me to have men and women on my terms and my conditions. It means I can have the sex life I want without the restrictions of being tied to a partner in a monogamous relationship. It lets me be me.*

Beatrice: *It's something we've always done and I can't see we're ever going to stop.*

Caroline: *I lived without swinging for twenty years. I could go back to the way things were if I had to. But I know I'd miss it.*

Dorothy: *I do it because it gives me exactly what I want. It's fun and exciting and every night is different. It's not a lifestyle that suits everyone. It's a lifestyle that can really hurt some people if they've not got the right attitude. But, for me, it's the only way to live.*